26/3/08.

Dear Warren

On behalf of

we wish you

+ thankyou for a job well done.

cheers.

AUSTRALIA**TODAY**

AUSTRALIA**TODAY**

A JOYOUS CELEBRATION
OF WHO WE ARE

RANDOM HOUSE AUSTRALIA

CONTENTS

We may not wake up each day and think about where we live, but there would be few Australians who don't know those first lines of Dorothea Mackellar's iconic poem: 'I love a sunburnt country, a land of sweeping plains …' Few of us who wouldn't know of the campaign to have 'Waltzing Matilda' installed as the national anthem. And few returning expats who are not moved by a glimpse of the sparkling coast or rugged inland through the windows of the flying kangaroo, made all the more evocative thanks to Peter Allen's 'I still call Australia home' echoing in their ears. These artistic examples of patriotism reveal our collective consciousness. For all our larrikin nature, there is a part of our psyche that is deeply nostalgic about what it means to be 'Australian'.

We are an adventurous race, forever leaving these shores for new experiences. This doesn't alter the fact that we are passionate about our people and our land. *Australia Today* celebrates this: who we are right now, the rich, diverse culture we've created, and the wealth of manmade and natural wonders that surround us. In this book, we travel state by state, capturing snapshots of the people and places that make this country what it is. We look at each state's history and its current status; the local legends and colourful characters; the diverse cities and their landmarks, suburbs, restaurants, shopping spots and open spaces; our famous beach lifestyle; the wide open country, with its towns, shows and produce; our quintessential sporting people, places and events; the eclectic arts and festivals; and, of course, the world-famous flora and fauna.

Whether you were born here or came from overseas, whether you live in the city or the bush, in the heat of the north or the cool of the south, or whether you see the sun rise over the water or over the desert, *Australia Today* is all about you – and for you.

New South Wales calls itself the Premier State because it was Australia's first colony. New South Welshmen and women also like to think that it remains first in terms of its economy, liveability and influence on greater Australia and the world. But it's a daily struggle to stay in front as its pesky younger siblings do their very best to knock the first-born bully off its perch.

NEW SOUTH WALES

Commuters enjoying a late-afternoon journey to Circular Quay on the famous **Manly Ferry**.

STATE**FILE**

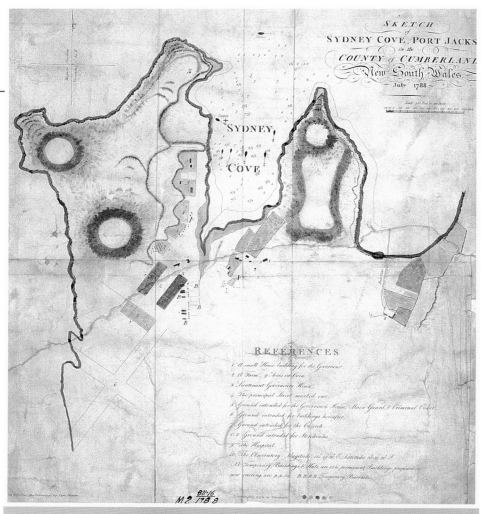

A plan for **Sydney Cove** in the 'County of Cumberland', dating from July 1788, marking a 'small house building for the Governor', the hospital, 'the principal Street', and the 'Ground intended for the buildings hereafter'.

W hen New South Wales was founded in 1788, it was inhabited by indigenous tribes and a motley collection of convicts, settlers and navy men. It was small in population but huge in size – it originally comprised most of Australia, basically everything east of Alice Springs. This perhaps accounts for the state's continuing sense of importance.

New South Wales was born on January 26, 1788, when Captain Phillip moored the First Fleet at Port Jackson and decided it would be the best place to build a colony with his convict charges.

The early days of the colony weren't easy. Food was scarce, crop cultivation proved difficult and the convicts were surly workers. By the 1790s, when Governor Bligh was trying to clean up the corrupt rum trade of the NSW Corps, the colony resembled an anarchical prison camp.

When Bligh was overthrown by officers in what became known as the Rum Rebellion, the British decided they needed a strong man to reform the wayward colonists. That man was Governor Macquarie, a hard but fair disciplinarian who arrived in 1809. He straightened out the state's inhabitants and commissioned the construction of roads, wharves, churches and public buildings in Sydney, where his planning influence can still be seen today. He also sent explorers across the country to open up the state's interior.

The colony changed in character again in the mid-19th century when the gold rush boosted the population by more than 30 per cent.

New South Wales was soon showing signs of maturity, and demanded self-government, which was finally granted with the Constitution Act of 1855.

The state thrived until the Depression of the 1930s, when the completion of construction of the Sydney Harbour Bridge was the only fillip to an otherwise beleaguered state. New South Wales surged again, at least economically, during the sad days of World War II, when industry boomed and unemployment was eliminated.

But it was not until the post-war period that the state began to take on its modern character. The 1960s brought the controversial – but ultimately and undoubtedly magnificent – construction of the Sydney Opera House, a world-class arts mecca, and the floods of post-war European migrants gave the state a reputation for ethnic and cultural diversity which continues today.

An early painting of the developing **Sydney Cove**.

DID YOU KNOW?

The area around Sydney Harbour was originally occupied by the Eora, Guringai and Daruk nations. There are some 2000 Aboriginal rock engraving sites in the Sydney area, and many suburbs have Aboriginal names, such as Bondi (meaning 'loud noise'), Parramatta ('eel creek') and Coogee ('smell').

The First Fleet comprised 11 ships. Although 1420 people, mostly convicts, embarked, only 1373 landed at Port Jackson. During the voyage there were 22 births and 69 people deserted, were discharged or died.

No one knows whether the state was named as a new South Wales or as a new Wales in the southern hemisphere.

Early European settlers thought that the Blue Mountains, to Sydney's west, were impenetrable until Blaxland, Wentworth and Lawson crossed them in 1813.

VITAL STATISTICS

NICKNAMES:	the Premier State, the First State
AREA:	809,444 km^2 (5th)
POPULATION:	6,817,100 (1st)
POPULATION DENSITY:	8.45 per km^2 (3rd)
LANDMARKS:	Byron Bay, Hunter Valley, Sydney Harbour Bridge, Sydney Opera House, the Three Sisters
MAIN INDUSTRIES:	business and financial services, information and communications technology, minerals production, agriculture and manufacturing
SPORTS:	rugby league, rugby union, AFL, cricket, netball, soccer, basketball
NATIONAL PARKS:	139 including Cape Byron, Jervis Bay, Kosciuszko, Nightcap, Ku-ring-gai Chase
WORLD HERITAGE SITES:	Lord Howe Island Group, Greater Blue Mountains Area, Willandra Lakes Region

NEWSOUTHWALESTODAY

This is a state that has never doubted its own importance. As the biggest in terms of population and trade, and as home to Australia's largest and most celebrated city, New South Wales is happy to label itself the 'Premier State' – it even says so on its numberplates.

The state's population is more than 6.8 million, and of that about 60 per cent live in the Sydney region. Most of the rest live in the two other major coastal cities, Newcastle and Wollongong, making it one of the more urbanised of Australia's states.

And New South Wales is set to get even more crowded. By 2025 it is projected that the population will grow to around 8 million, with Sydney to remain the main population centre. Regional areas are expected to experience a decline in population, as even more people move to the cities for jobs and opportunities.

You can't deny how much New South Wales puts into the economy. Sydney alone contributes around a quarter of the entire

SIGNS OF GOVERNMENT

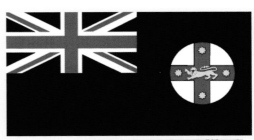

The New South Wales **coat of arms**, formally adopted in 1906, shows the British Lion in the Southern Cross, with symbols of agriculture in its corners. The coat of arms is supported by the British Lion and the Australian Kangaroo and features the NSW motto 'Newly risen, how brightly you shine'.

The British Lion and Southern Cross appear again on the **state flag**, next to the Union Jack. The flag has been in use since 1876.

Parliament House is the oldest public building in Sydney. Inside, the chambers of the Legislative Assembly and Council are painted green and red respectively, reflecting the colour schemes of the British House of Commons and House of Lords.

gross domestic product. Most of the nation's media is concentrated here, including PBL, the Seven and Nine networks, and Fairfax. The city is also the epicentre of the communications and finance industries. The Australian Stock Exchange and the Reserve Bank of Australia are located in Sydney, as are the headquarters of more than 90 banks. Tourism is, of course, another big money earner.

Outside the city, agriculture doesn't contribute as much to the economy as it used to, but is still very important. New South Wales is the country's largest producer of rice, maize, oranges and cotton, among other crops. Minerals are also key, with coal accounting for 80 per cent of production, and China becoming an increasingly important customer.

Physically, the state is diverse. It has about 1900 kilometres of coastline and some of the best surf breaks in the country, but also boasts the Snowy Mountain range, and the semi-desert regions beyond Bourke. It's also an ancient land, something you can easily imagine at places like Lake Mungo, where the 40,000-year-old Mungo Man was discovered, or the bizarre, prehistoric rock formations of the Warrumbungles, in the state's north-west.

NATURAL AMBASSADORS

The spectacular red **waratah** is protected by law. Its name comes from the Eora language and is now shared by the NSW rugby team.

The **kookaburra**, a member of the kingfisher family, is sometimes called a 'laughing jackass' because of its distinctive territorial call.

With its webbed feet and duck-like bill, the **platypus** is one of the world's few monotremes (mammals that lay eggs and can detect electric fields around prey). Although they look cute, males have a spur on their back foot that can inject a painful venom.

The **blue groper** was proclaimed the state marine animal of New South Wales in 1998. Known to be powerful but curious, this friendly fish often follows divers.

PEOPLEFILE

They call them 'cockroaches'. It's a name that started with State of Origin rugby, when it seemed appropriate to name the opposition after their most prevalent pests. It's not an altogether affectionate nickname either; the citizens of New South Wales, most of whom live in the cities, have a reputation for scurrying around looking for crumbs of money, caring little for the rest of the country and living life at a much faster pace. Of course, they would say that the other states are just jealous.

Jogging in leafy **Centennial Park**, Sydney.

Schoolkids: **the multicultural face** of New South Wales.

MOST LIKELY TO SAY:

How much did your house go for?

What, not more fireworks over the harbour?

I don't have to cross the Bridge, do I?

LEAST LIKELY TO SAY:

Harbour views are overrated, anyway.

The 2000 Olympics were the worst two weeks of my life.

I really hate the beach – all that sand!

NSW people are mostly urban creatures, and they like it that way. Their cities have so much to offer, why would they ever want to leave? They have the highest per capita income of all the states, and they like to spend it, whether it's on a house with a harbour view, a world-class dining experience or a pair of Sass & Bide jeans.

More than anything, though, the state can be defined by its cosmopolitan flavour. The population boom began after World War II, when Prime Minister Billy Hughes said we must 'populate or perish'. The state received the lion's share of new arrivals, a mixture of 'Ten-pound Poms' and displaced European immigrants.

Some weren't so happy when they arrived and saw the make-shift camps they were to stay in. One British migrant recounted to *The Sydney Morning Herald* that his wife broke down and wept: 'But that was only the first impression … she is alright today,' he said. As were most of the migrants, who settled in and brought the cultures of their homelands with them.

Today almost a quarter of New South Welshmen were born overseas, nearly 20 per cent speak a language other than English at home, and a stroll through Sydney's Chinatown, the street markets of Cabramatta or the Italian restaurants of the Riverina district leaves you in no doubt as to the authenticity of the state's ethnic mix.

NSW people are mostly urban creatures, and they like it that way.

LIVINGLARGE

New South Wales has produced heroes and villains, politicians and eccentrics, authors and artists, great scientists and philanthropists. But the state is perhaps proudest of its criminals, unsurprising when you consider its convict history.

Bushranger Ben Hall was one of the first and one of the best. Born in Maitland in the Hunter Valley, Ben Hall started out as a fairly successful grazier near Forbes, but was lured by another notable bushranger, Frank Gardiner, to a more exciting career in highway robbery.

Hall's biggest hold-up was when he robbed the gold escort coach near Eugowra Rocks of more than 14,000 pounds in gold and banknotes. He was eventually shot by police in 1865. Despite his violent exploits, Hall is remembered as a chivalrous and gentlemanly bushranger, and is immortalised in bush ballads and street names throughout the state.

Other early European settlers undertook the more honest work of the state. When Lieutenant John Macarthur was granted his first 100 acres of farmland in the Parramatta area, he saw an opportunity to produce more than just food for the growing colony. He imported

With their skimpy swimmers and red and yellow caps, it's hard to miss **Bondi's lifesavers** – everyday heroes.

Come all ye wild colonials and listen to my tale;
A story of bushrangers' deeds I will to you unveil.
'Tis of those gallant heroes, game fighters one and all;
And we'll sit and sing, Long Live the King, Dunn, Gilbert, and Ben Hall.

From *The Ballad of Ben Hall's Gang.*

COLOURFUL CHARACTERS

The Eternity Man born in 1884 in the Balmain slums, Arthur Malcolm Stace became a state ward at the age of 12 and began drinking from an early age. He was jailed at 15 and in his 20s became a look-out for his sister's brothels. However, Stace found God in 1930. He became enamoured with the idea of eternity, and saw it as his calling to spread God's word.

From 1932 onwards, Sydneysiders started to see the word 'Eternity' chalked on their streets in perfect copperplate script, but no one ever saw who was responsible. The mystery continued until 1956, when the Reverend Lisle M Thompson, the preacher at the church where Stace worked as a cleaner, saw him write the word on the footpath. The Reverend wrote an article about 'Mr Eternity' for the *Sydney Sunday Telegraph* and the name stuck.

Stace died in a nursing home at the age of 83, but his life's work was immortalised when the Harbour Bridge was lit up with the word 'Eternity' for the millennium New Year's Eve celebrations.

Abe Saffron believe it or not, notorious Kings Cross was once considered to be one of Sydney's most prestigious areas. By the turbulent 1960s, however, it was the city's main tourism, entertainment and red-light district. Nightclub owner Abe Saffron was known as 'the boss of the Cross' and once sued a newspaper for using his other nickname – Mr Sin.

Saffron's career began after the war, when he became involved in an infamous Kings Cross nightclub called The Roosevelt Club. He took full advantage of the area's growing notoriety and popularity, and within a few years he owned a string of nightclubs, strip joints and sex shops, most notably Les Girls, which gave Sydneysiders one of their first transvestite revues. Despite rumours of numerous illegal activities, including the sale of illegal grog and even murder, Saffron wasn't convicted of any crimes until 1987, when he was jailed for tax evasion.

his first merino sheep from Spain in 1796 and with his wife, Elizabeth, effectively pioneered Australia's wool industry. Less than ten years later, Gregory Blaxland, William Wentworth and William Charles Lawson further expanded the colony's agricultural potential when they became the first white men to cross the seemingly impenetrable Blue Mountains.

Sir Henry Parkes and Edmund Barton, Australia's 'fathers of Federation', were both New South Welshmen, as are some of the country's most notable arts figures, from the poet and journalist Dame Mary Gilmore to Nobel Prize winner Patrick White and playwright David Williamson.

In the 20th century, the state also produced great science and medicine men. Sir Ian Clunies-Ross was the first chair of the CSIRO, and Dr Fred Hollows was the ophthalmologist who helped thousands of people across the state to regain their vision. Together with the activist 'Mum' Shirl Smith, Hollows set up the Aboriginal Medical Service in Redfern, Sydney.

But sometimes the best heroes are the everyday ones. Bondi's professional lifeguards and volunteer lifesavers are some of the country's most recognised. With up to 30,000 visitors to the beach in a summer's day, it's not unusual for them to perform up to 100 rescues – that's 20 to 30 per lifeguard.

History meets the future at majestic **Sydney University**.

CITYSTYLE

Since former Olympics supremo Juan Antonio Samaranch mispronounced the city's name as he announced the winning bid for the 2000 Olympic Games, 'Syderney' hasn't looked back.

If the world didn't know Sydney's Opera House, Harbour Bridge and Bondi Beach before the Games – which were beamed to an estimated 3.6 billion people and which Samaranch dubbed the 'best ever' – they do now.

In the UK, they watch a reality TV series about Bondi's lifeguards. Backpackers everywhere swap stories of red lights and late-night kebabs in the party precinct of Kings Cross. And as TV news programs report on global New Year's Eve celebrations, they invariably cross to pictures of fireworks exploding above the Opera House and the Harbour Bridge and to the now-traditional surprise graphic that lights up on the Bridge's Coathanger span.

For Sydneysiders, the city's landmarks are both a source of pride and part of day-to-day life. Each weekday sees ferries criss-crossing the harbour, carrying tourists and commuters on over 35,000 trips, while on weekends the waters are packed with jetboats, kayaks, fishing boats and yachts. The iconic white sails of the Opera House serve as a regular backdrop for craft markets, picnics in the Botanic Gardens or major cultural events, such as the final performance of Channel Ten's *Australian Idol*. The cost of pride can be high, however: the cost of building the Opera House was originally estimated at $3 million, but eventually soared to a massive $102 million, and still hasn't been finished according to its Danish architect Joern Utzon's plans.

Sydney's skyline, long dominated by Sydney Tower and the late architect Harry Seidler's MLC Centre and Australia Square building – which any Sydneysider will tell you is, in fact, circular – has been augmented in recent times by international luminaries such as Renzo Piano and Lord Norman Foster; look for the sky-high set of footy goalposts on the Deutsche Bank building.

The Archibald Fountain in **Hyde Park**, the green heart of a city filled with skyscrapers.

View across the rides of **Luna Park** (main picture) to the Sydney Harbour Bridge and Opera House.

Old and new: a tall ship (above, top) sails past the **Sydney Opera House**.

Government House (immediately above), once the Governor's residence, is set amongst the flowerbeds of the Royal Botanic Gardens.

75YEARSOFTHEBRIDGE

The **Sydney Harbour Bridge** under construction, about 1929–30.

'Wanted: the sabre that rattled a premier and astonished a city.' That was one of the ads placed in the world's media by Harbour Bridge fanatic Paul Cave during his 18-year search for the sword used by the right-wing ratbag Francis De Groot. De Groot, a World War I cavalry soldier, stole the thunder at the 1932 opening of the Sydney Harbour Bridge by slashing the ribbon before NSW Premier Jack Lang could do so with a pair of scissors. But De Groot later returned to his native Ireland and the sword was lost.

In 1998, after years of lobbying, Cave convinced authorities to turn the Coathanger into a tourist attraction and launched the BridgeClimb company. In the lead-up to the Bridge's 75th anniversary in 2007, he finally located the sword, bought it for a 'significant amount' at auction, and returned it to Sydney where it featured in the party and is now raising money for cancer research. Sydney's *Daily Telegraph* newspaper described it as 'as much a part of Harbour Bridge legend as Excalibur is to Camelot'.

The blade's homecoming was just one of hundreds of Bridge stories that emerged in the lead-up to the anniversary. Sydneysiders told of how they had been born on the Bridge, had their first kiss on it, climbed it illegally and popped the question atop it.

An estimated 200,000 of them walked across it to mark the milestone, which was more than the 160,000 vehicles that cross it on an average day. The walkers on Sunday 18 March, a day before the real anniversary, included descendants of Lang and the Bridge's chief engineer John Bradfield, and descendants of the 16 men who died during its construction.

On the same day, the Bridge joined its sidekick, the Sydney Opera House, on the National Heritage List.

On 18 March 2007, thousands of Sydneysiders and others from all over Australia walked across the Bridge to celebrate its **75th birthday**.

BRIDGE NUMBERS

Vehicles per day, on average: 160,000

Proposals per week at the peak: 2

Metres of roadway: 503 from pylon to pylon

Height: 134 metres

Weight: 52,800 tonnes

Peak number of workers employed on the bridge: 1654

Rivets used in construction: 6 million

Years it took to build: 7

Number of locomotives parked on it to test it before opening in 1932: 50

STATUS, SUBSTANCE, SIN

Former Prime Minister Paul Keating once said, 'If you're not in Sydney, you're just camping out.'

From its birthplace in what is now known as Circular Quay, Australia's biggest city has spread from the Hawkesbury River in the north, to the Royal National Park in the south, the Blue Mountains in the west and the Pacific Ocean to the east. It's home to more than 4 million people, but, due to low land values in its early years, people were able to spread out and now enjoy a fair amount of living space.

Drive outwards from the first sandstone cottages in The Rocks district, quarried from nearby Pyrmont and home to pubs and tourist shops, and you can see how the city has sprawled over two centuries, from the inner-city Victorian terraces of Woolloomooloo, Paddington and Balmain, to the grand Federation houses and Californian bungalows of Haberfield, Chatswood, Rose Bay and Kensington.

It was the introduction of trains in the 1870s that kicked off the urban sprawl – and the arrival of cars in the 1950s that made it an explosion. Today, the owner/builders of the so-called 'McMansions' in Sydney's newest suburbs to the south-west and north-west are the nation's political kingmakers. Often labelled 'Howard's battlers' or 'the aspirational classes', they are Australia's political middle and they decide who rules in the NSW and Canberra corridors of power.

Paul Keating once said, 'If you're not in Sydney, you're just camping out.'

Sydney's skyline (above), seen from Circular Quay. Building façades on **Macquarie Street** (below).

LOCAL LEGENDS

In a city fascinated by real estate, there's no hotter topic than the development of historic buildings. One infamous battle between the developers and preservation crusaders involved a bohemian heiress, **Juanita Nielsen**. Her mysterious disappearance in 1975 followed her campaign to protect the majestic buildings of Woolloomooloo, Potts Point and Kings Cross. An inquest failed to resolve her almost-certain murder, but threw suspicion on some of the country's most notorious criminals and exposed corruption throughout the police force. However, her death wasn't in vain; her work led to the passing of tighter, new planning laws, and Victoria Street has retained many of its heritage-listed buildings.

The **Finger Wharf** at Woolloomooloo (above), home to the rich and famous, as well as a selection of top restaurants.

Classic terrace houses (left) in Union Street, **Paddington**.

HOT**PROPERTY**

As the playwright David Williamson notes in his play *Emerald City*, Melburnians agonise over the meaning of life, but Sydneysiders already know what it is: a harbour view.

A million dollars no longer buys much harbour in the Emerald City. To keep up with the Joneses, the Packers and the Murdochs in the city's more desirable locales, you're likely to need something like $50 million – or more.

Multi-million-dollar views from the waterfront mansions in exclusive Wolseley Road, **Point Piper**.

The exotic sunroom of Elizabeth Bay's most famous house, **Boomerang**.

2007. The 4770-square metre Hopetoun Avenue block they were after contains three houses: one clifftop residence and two Timothy Moon-designed guesthouses on the Middle Harbour foreshore.

At the time, the record amount paid for a Sydney home was a measly $28 million. Publisher Deke Miskin and his wife Eve shelled this out to buy Point Piper's iconic Altona from Fiona Handbury, the ex-wife of Rupert Murdoch's nephew Matt Handbury, in 2002.

Real estate agents now routinely field offers of $50 million for Altona and the house alongside it, the castle of recruiter Andrew Banks and wife Andrea. But both owners, said veteran Eastern Suburbs real estate agent Bill Bridges in January 2007, will only consider offers above $65 million.

Closer to the CBD, the once-industrial Finger Wharf at Woolloomooloo has, like most of inner Sydney, been gentrified to the point where Hollywood bad boy and rugby league club owner Russell Crowe has decided to move in, upstairs from 'the Golden Tonsils', radio legend John Laws.

Thanks to a post-war property boom, Sydney today doesn't just have rich people. It has the rich, the nouveau riche and the nouveau, nouveau riche.

In the early 1990s, the median house price was $150,000. It's now more than $500,000 and tipped to reach seven figures by 2012. Even $50 million wasn't enough for one recent cashed-up buyer, whose offer for the Balmoral home of food importer Roy Manassen and his wife Cindy was reportedly knocked back in early

> Sydney today doesn't just have rich people. It has the rich, the nouveau riche and the nouveau, nouveau riche.

WHERE'S HOT, WHERE'S NOT

Although the harbour is home to the old money, the newer generation of billionaires prefers **the beach**. James Packer, Australia's richest man since the death of father Kerry in 2005, lives in Bondi. Lachlan Murdoch and wife Sarah live in Bronte. Hollywood hunk Heath Ledger lived there too, until he grew tired of the lurking lenses of the paparazzi and moved to New York.

It's not easy to find a suburb where people don't want to live in Sydney, but only the most resilient can live in Tempe, where aircraft noise from the city's all-too-central airport soars to 85 decibels. And spare a thought for the 47 inhabitants of Kerslake, a unit block that fell into a hole 10 metres wide and 10 metres deep when the Lane Cove Tunnel collapsed beneath it during construction in 2005. Fortunately, no residents were injured. Even Tweety the pet cockatiel made it out alive, thanks to the rescue efforts of a bomb-squad robot.

DESIGNERHEAVEN

'If Sydney was personified, she'd be bronzed, brazen and almost certainly wearing a Zimmermann bikini ...'

Top model Miranda Kerr on the runway for Zimmermann during **Australian Fashion Week**.

... so suggested journalist Anthea Loucas in *The Sydney Morning Herald*, but Sydney's interest in style goes way beyond 'sunny swimwear'. In a city with a keen sense of style, shopping comes a close third to eating and drawing breath. The city's shops are the best place to see and be seen.

'A Temple of Affluenza' is what the left-wing commentator Clive Hamilton calls Sydney's newest mega-mall in Bondi Junction, where cashed-up shoppers – or those with credit cards, anyhow – flock to worship at the altar of fashion.

But it's water off a sartorial duck's back. In the malls of Parramatta, Miranda, Eastgardens and Burwood, teenagers congregate to shop, watch movies and flirt, while fashionistas drop in to find a Saturday night outfit, quickly.

With more time on their hands, shoppers might venture into the CBD to hunt through the high-street fashions of Pitt Street Mall and the Queen Victoria Building, rifle through the designer clothes of David Jones and Myer, or take a turn down the Victorian Strand Arcade, where some of the city's most established couturiers hang their creations alongside its newest talents in the Fashion Design Studio's The Graduate Store.

For the truly dedicated follower of fashion, though, there's no substitute for a stroll through the rarefied streets of Paddington and Woollahra. Collette Dinnigan, Sass & Bide, Lisa Ho, Ksubi, Leona Edmiston, Dinosaur Designs. They're all from Sydney, darling, and they all have shops here, provided you know where to look.

Try a stroll down Glenmore Road, through Five Ways, onto Jersey Road, Queen Street and back down Oxford Street for an afternoon that will take in the designers above, as well as Bare by Rebecca Davies, Kitten, Easton Pearson and Akira Isogawa. If you simply can't decide what's in and what's out, take a right off Oxford Street and ask the notoriously discerning fashion guru Belinda Seper at her shops on William Street.

Of course, if you trust your own eye, you'll go straight to the weekend markets of Paddington and Bondi, where the Dinnigans, Hos and Willows once plied their trade at a fraction of the price, or you might hit the op shops, formerly the domain of charities such as St Vincent de Paul and The Salvation Army, that rode the 1990s retro revival and are now in most inner-city and beachside suburbs, filled with handpicked and handsomely priced relics of the designers of the 50s, 60s and 70s.

Alex Perry
Alice McCall
Camilla and Marc
Carla Zampatti
Fleur Wood
Ginger & Smart
Jayson Brunsdon
Josh Goot
Kirrily Johnston
Leona Edmiston
Lisa Ho
Nicola Finetti
Sass & Bide
Willow
Yeojin Bae
Zimmermann

World-renowned designer **Collette Dinnigan** in her Sydney store.

ROOMWITHAVIEW

In spite of its beginnings as a colony of Britain – which gave the world the Yorkshire pudding – four main factors have conspired to make Sydney a top-shelf place to eat: foodie pioneers, wave after wave of 'new Australians', stunning views and great produce.

Gay and Tony Bilson, Sydney's first celebrity chefs, opened the Berowra Waters Inn in 1977 and closed it in 1995, training half of Sydney's future food stars in the interim. With other pioneers, they begged, borrowed and stole recipes and ingredients from the fresh seafood, meat, fruit and vegetables available in Australia and combines them using a mixture of techniques from around the world. At Aria, which steals its name from the Opera House next door, you might order a dozen freshly shucked Sydney rock oysters served with a Japanese ponzu dressing or Western Australian scampi wrapped in a Tunisian brick pastry. Or at the Icebergs Dining Room overlooking Bondi Beach, you could go for Tallabung pork from the state's central west with Italian 'pepperoni mandorlati' (pan-roasted yellow peppers).

The opulent members only room, De Nom, at **Ruby Rabbit** (above). **Firefly Wine Bar** (right) at Walsh Bay.

indigenous Australians as well as all the Europeans, Asians and Arabs who have been arriving here since World War II and who usually make Sydney their first stop.

The result was something called Modern Australian cuisine, a United Nations approach to cooking that is nothing more than a label for any dish someone decides to throw together in Australia today.

At its best, Mod Oz takes advantage of the impressive variety of

At its most basic, Mod Oz is a meat pie with mushy peas and gravy from Harry's Café de Wheels, the harbourside caravan at Woolloomooloo, which is open all hours and has cured the late-night munchies of generations of sailors, drinkers and shift workers.

As at Aria, Icebergs and Harry's, most Sydney food comes with the option of eating outdoors and a killer view of the water, either the Pacific Ocean, the harbour or one of the rivers that feed it. It's comforting to know that when a Mod Oz experiment goes horribly

The magnificent ocean views (and memorable cocktails) at Bondi Beach's **Icebergs Dining Room & Bar**

BEROWRA BABIES

The supermodels of the noughties, celebrity chefs have spread far beyond the kitchen, appearing in toothpaste advertisements, Qantas brochures and, well, even with the odd supermodel. According to food writer Scott Bolles, a handful of Sydney restaurants began a foodie revolution in the 1980s, which gave the place its obsession with chefs. Take the Berowra Waters Inn, for example:

Anders Ousback the late chef went on to establish Dov in Darlinghurst and the Clock Hotel restaurant.

Janni Kyritsis went on to open MG Garage, which scored three chef's hats in its first year of opening.

Paul Merrony graduated to Merrony's, where **Guillaume Brahimi** worked before moving to Quay and then opening Guillaume at Bennelong at the Opera House.

Neil Perry most famous for his Rockpool restaurant, Neil got his start with Berowra old-boy **Michael McMahon**, who now has Catalina in Rose Bay.

wrong, in Sydney at least, there's usually something nice to look at. The only thing that moves faster than the restaurant landscape in Sydney is the nightlife. By the time you've heard of the newest bar or nightclub in Sydney, chances are the hip crowd has moved on to the next one as Sin City's hoteliers try to outdo one another for the notoriously fickle attentions of its beautiful people.

At Favela, in Kings Cross, they spent millions on the décor, recreating a lighting effect of globes that pulse in time to the music, which the club's owner once saw on a night out in Amsterdam. At De Nom, the private members' room above Ruby Rabbit nightclub, they recreated the decadence of the Palace of Versailles.

When it comes to Sydney pubs and bars, the theme is definitely 'bigger is better'. The high cost of liquor licences in NSW means most of the capital's watering holes are owned by one of its 'pokie kings' and 'bar tzars', such as hotels godfather Arthur Laundy or the racecar-driving playboy Justin Hemmes. In the state that once was home to the Rum Rebellion, a revolution fuelled by enforced sobriety, they're unlikely to go broke anytime soon.

SUPERSTAR**RESTAURANT**

The Japanese may have a reputation for sticking to tradition – but Tetsuya Wakuda certainly doesn't heed stereotypes. It was an enterprising, some might say very Australian, spirit that not only led him to Sydney from Japan in 1982 with nothing more than a limited grasp of English and a love of food, but also inspires his groundbreaking dishes.

Tetsuya is also known for being dignified and humble, again going against the cliché – this time a culinary one. As this master of cuisine modestly says, 'I made a lot of things up along the way, and luckily for me, people liked the way it tasted.'

After initially slogging it as a kitchenhand, Tetsuya sliced a path through the field to open his eponymous restaurant in 1989. This tiny hole-in-the-wall in Sydney's Rozelle was booked out daily. In 2000 he moved to his current location, a gracious old building in Kent Street in the CBD, where guests can choose private dining rooms or the main restaurant overlooking a Japanese garden, and where he has his own 'experimentation' kitchen, and pursues his Japanese philosophy of using natural seasonal flavours and the freshest ingredients, enhanced by classic French technique.

Tetsuya has refined his reputation to become one of Australia's, if not the world's, most renowned – if reluctant – celebrity chefs. His awards list is lengthy, to say the least: the restaurant consistently earns three hats in *The Sydney Morning Herald's Good Food Guide*, and in April of 2007, it was ranked the fifth best eatery in

The man himself: **Tetsuya** at his restaurant.

He uses the freshest ingredients to prepare **roulade of garfish**.

the world by the industry's respected *Restaurant* magazine, up with El Bulli in Spain and The Fat Duck in the UK. Tetsuya's signature dish, confit of Petuna Tasmanian ocean trout with konbu, daikon and fennel, is on the must-eat list of gourmands everywhere, and diners think nothing of forking out $185 for his degustation menu.

These days, you're most likely to spot the quietly spoken chef hanging out in Tassie with his good mate – and now local resident – arts critic Leo Schofield. Here Tetsuya's island heritage, love for organic produce and natural humility ensure that he blends in.

'I made a lot of things up along the way, and luckily for me, people liked the way it tasted.'

THE EXPERIMENTATION MENU ...

Hors d'oeuvres may include:

Gazpacho with spiced tomato sorbet

West Australian marron with asparagus and truffle mayonnaise

Tartare of tuna with fresh wasabi

Marinated fillet of trevally with preserved lemon set on sushi rice

Tataki of venison with rosemary and honey

Pea soup with bitter chocolate sorbet

Smoked ocean trout and avruga caviar

Leek and crab custard

Scallop carpaccio with red wine vinaigrette

The signature dish (and other tastes) follows:

Confit of Petuna Tasmanian ocean trout with konbu, daikon and fennel

Ravioli of Queensland spanner crab with tomato and basil vinaigrette

Grilled fillet of barramundi with braised nameko, enoki and woodear mushrooms

Twice cooked de-boned spatchcock with olive and caper jus

Grilled wagyu beef with lime and wasabi

Comte with lentils

Desserts may include:

Orange, honey and black pepper sorbet

Blue cheese bavarois

Early season berries with orange and Grand Marnier jelly and champagne ice cream

Flourless chocolate cake with a bitter chocolate sorbet and orange ice cream

Vanilla bean ice cream with white beans and dates

Chocolate terrine with mascarpone and cognac Anglaise

OPENSPACES, SECRETRETREATS

The national anthem tells us that our home is 'girt by sea'. Although they wouldn't often drop the word 'girt' into everyday conversations, it's doubly true for Sydneysiders: both their nation and their city are surrounded by water.

Sydney has the aqua-trifecta of ocean beaches, calm coves and a broad, deep harbour, with the added appeal of being bordered by national parks, so it's little surprise that, while Melbourne might lay claim to being Australia's sporting and cultural capital and Adelaide its epicurean centre, Sydney is very much the outdoors type.

Her beaches can be divided into three groups: the less crowded northern beaches along the 'insular peninsula', stretching from the North Head of the harbour to the exclusive Palm Beach; the crammed, glam city beaches from Bondi down to Maroubra; and the southern beaches lined up along a single, long stretch between Botany Bay and Cronulla. Councils provide popular coin-operated barbeques in the parks behind most beaches, which draw queues on busy Saturdays and Sundays in summer. Some of them even work!

If they're not holding the tongs and turning the snags, Sydneysiders can often be found picnicking at parks such as Hyde, Centennial or Bicentennial in the city. The Royal Botanic Gardens, with their majestic Moreton Bay figs and noisy resident fruit bats, are a particularly good space for a walk. They were founded by Governor Macquarie in 1816, making them the oldest scientific institution in Australia. Further afield you'll find the Royal National Park to the south and Ku-ring-gai Chase National Park to the north.

If they're the sporting type, Sydneysiders might be found enjoying a quasi-holiday on the metropolitan fringe: trying not to get lost bushwalking in the World Heritage-listed beauty of the Blue Mountains, dodging Australia's last riverboat postman as they waterski on the Hawkesbury River, or sailing on Pittwater, Port Hacking or Botany Bay.

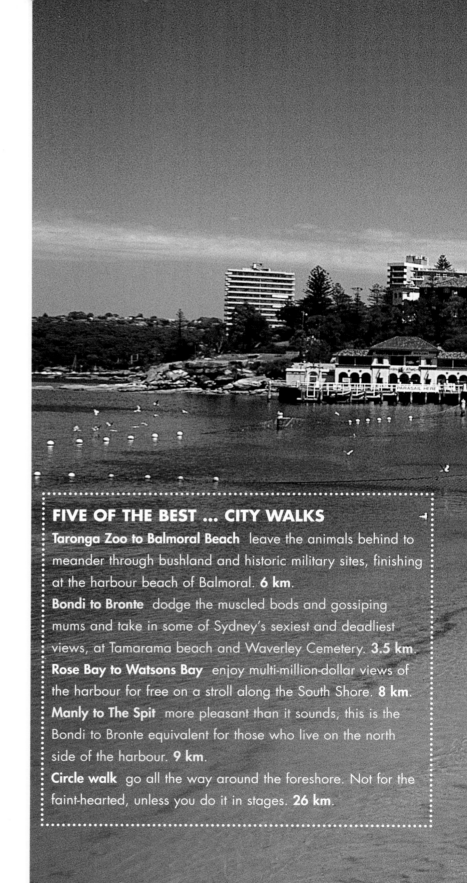

FIVE OF THE BEST ... CITY WALKS

Taronga Zoo to Balmoral Beach leave the animals behind to meander through bushland and historic military sites, finishing at the harbour beach of Balmoral. **6 km.**

Bondi to Bronte dodge the muscled bods and gossiping mums and take in some of Sydney's sexiest and deadliest views, at Tamarama beach and Waverley Cemetery. **3.5 km.**

Rose Bay to Watsons Bay enjoy multi-million-dollar views of the harbour for free on a stroll along the South Shore. **8 km.**

Manly to The Spit more pleasant than it sounds, this is the Bondi to Bronte equivalent for those who live on the north side of the harbour. **9 km.**

Circle walk go all the way around the foreshore. Not for the faint-hearted, unless you do it in stages. **26 km.**

Sydney has the aqua-trifecta of
ocean beaches, calm coves
and a broad, deep harbour.

The sheltered **harbour beach** at Manly
(main picture) is a favourite with families.

A pagoda in Darling Harbour's **Chinese
Gardens** (inset).

BEACHLIVING

When the rag-tag crew of the First Fleet saw its first NSW beaches, Botany Bay and the sandy coves of Port Jackson, they no doubt appreciated their beauty, but they probably never imagined how great a role beach living would play in the later life of their new colony.

Out for an early-morning walk beside **Coogee Beach**.

More than 200 years later, the state's beaches are its lungs – where New South Welshmen go to take a deep breath, spend time with family and blow off steam. Perhaps the state's most famous stretch of sand is Sydney's Bondi, with its mix of posers and surfers, locals and tourists, desperate to firm up those glutes or to catch a piece of Australian sunshine to take back home. But moving away from the city, the crowds and buildings thin out, allowing you to appreciate the natural beauty of the state's Pacific shore.

The northern coastline of New South Wales is synonymous with relaxation and sunshine. The beaches are simply beautiful, often fringed with bushland and offering some of the most spectacular views in the world. The jewel in the crown of the north is, of course, Byron Bay. Its elegantly sweeping bay culminates in stately Cape Byron, Australia's easternmost point, and is backed by an easygoing town, known the world over for its excellent surfing and vibrant, counter-culture lifestyle. Further south, Yamba, with its plethora of cafés, restaurants and day spas, has become one of the hippest towns on the coast. And just outside of Sydney, perfect for a weekend break, is the Central Coast, a stretch characterised by picturesque villages set in pretty bays and inlets.

Swim between the flags at world-famous **Bondi Beach**.

SEASCAPES: OCEAN BATHS

New South Wales's ribbon of **sparkling beaches** has given rise to that quintessential Australian architectural delight: the beach bath. With the most popular beaches often sporting several on one stretch, these salt-encrusted, seawater pools are a haven for lap swimmers and kids alike – not to mention the occasional visiting sea creature. Newcastle's Merewether Beach has a fine set of old-style pools, built into the rocks with a colourful Art Deco backdrop. Since they opened in 1935, they've become a favourite of artists, wedding parties and tourists.

Swimmers lap up the Mediterranean blues of **Bronte's** ocean baths.

The state's beaches are its lungs, where New South Welshmen go to take a deep breath ...

The beaches of the South Coast may not have world renown, but they certainly have windswept charm. Off the fine-sanded shores of Kiama, Mollymook or Narooma, swimmers often share the waves with pods of dolphins, and in the winter months the beaches are prime spots for whale watching. Surfers need more serious breaks, and they find them at Gerringong, Gerroa and the breathtaking Seven Mile Beach, so long it was used as a runway by Sir Charles Kingsford Smith as he set off on the first commercial flight from Australia to New Zealand in 1933.

The lighthouse at **Wollongong**.

A fish feeding frenzy at **Lord Howe Island** off the NSW coast.

FIVE OF THE BEST ... **NSW BEACHES**

Bermagui it was in the crystal clear waters of the southern Sapphire Coast that the American author Zane Grey helped to pioneer the sport of gamefishing in the 1930s.

Jervis Bay the beach is claimed by some to have the whitest sand in the world, but the area also boasts an interesting Aboriginal history and gorgeous clear blue waters.

Lennox Head just south of Byron Bay, Lennox Head has breathtaking views, especially from May to October when migratory humpback whales pass by.

North Narrabeen the surfing capital of Sydney, it's a great place to spot world champs in the making, curling through the waves.

Seal Rocks another surfers' favourite, nestled in lush national park. Nearby Sugarloaf Point lighthouse offers magnificent panoramic views.

BEACHPLAY

The shores of NSW are more than just decoration. Locals visit the beach daily for a variety of activities, from surfing at Angourie to fishing at Ulladulla.

Wollongong offers the only place in New South Wales where you can sky-dive to the beach, if you so choose, or its Bald Hill is also the place to try hang-gliding – beginners can go tandem. For those who are a bit more risk-averse, this is simply a great place to enjoy the magnificent views.

Bondi became famous for its beach volleyball culture when it hosted the sport during the Sydney Olympics in 2000, and since then the sport has taken off. Many surf lifesaving clubs along the coast now hire out volleyball nets for those beachgoers who want to combine their sunbathing with something a little more active.

Surf clubs such as Queenscliff and Coogee are also famous for their surf-boat races. Professional rescuers and amateur athletes train hard for this exciting sport, while plentiful thrills and spills make it a favourite with spectators at the regular competitions.

But perhaps the favourite beach pastime of New South Welshmen is people-watching. From the wizened old salts who swim the harbour pools of Sydney every day, winter through summer, to the bronzed beauties of Bondi and the hippies of Byron Bay, there is always something to see on the beaches of New South Wales.

THIS SURFING LIFE

In the 1970s, when the waves at Byron Bay were beginning to feel crowded, surfing legend and former world champion Nat Young searched for a new piece of paradise. He found it at **Angourie**, a stunning beach on the northern tip of the Yuragir National Park and arguably NSW's best surf break.

Once just a great surf spot with a few holiday cottages, the area now thrives on its reputation and spectacular ocean views. The famous Blue Pool, located in bush near the beach, was originally a quarry but it has since filled with fresh water and is perfect for swimming. There's also a special viewing platform, which means visitors can admire the surfers' abilities without getting wet.

In January 2007, Angourie was declared the state's first surfing reserve and became a protected area – a nod to what's surely one of our most popular national pastimes.

The ubiquitous surfers at **Byron**.

COUNTRY STYLE

NSW may be the most urban state, but its countryside is varied and beautiful. Move inland from the coast and you encounter the sweeping dairy pastures of the south or the sub-tropical north coast hinterland. Further west the grass thins out across empty plains, until you reach the striking red earth of the true outback, 'Back o' Bourke'.

When Blaxland, Wentworth and Lawson finally cut a path through the Blue Mountains in 1813, they had no idea of the potential of inland New South Wales. Squatters soon followed, securing themselves vast stretches of grazing land and, later, huge fortunes to match, from the country's burgeoning wool trade. But it was in 1851 that the land's hidden riches came to light, with the country's first major discovery of gold near Bathurst. The rush that followed brought wealth and hardship in unfair measure.

Those who come to Bathurst today have a much easier stay. Weekend visitors from Sydney browse the town's antique shops and stroll through its history-soaked streets. As Australia's oldest inland settlement, the town's streets are graced with wonderfully preserved 19th-century architecture. For those who live here, Bathurst is an important regional community at the heart of a pastoral, fruit- and grain-growing district.

A lusher type of country can be found in the north-east of the state. The Richmond River valley is one of most populated rural areas in Australia. Lismore is its main town. Established as a port for

The rolling hills of grazing land at **Kiama** (main picture).

Grafton's flowering jacaranda trees (above) in magnificent bloom.

The misty streets of **Gulgong** (right), an historic gold rush town.

the timber trade, forestry still feeds the local economy, but agriculture is also important. With the area's warm climate, bananas, sugar cane, avocados and tropical fruit can be grown. Coffee is a local speciality and is regularly consumed in Lismore's many cafés, frequented by tourists and the local artistic community alike.

For dry colonial character, head west. This is the mighty and mythical 'outback', littered with the ghosts of former mining towns. Despite their remoteness, however, some towns have survived. Henry Lawson once said, 'If you know Bourke, you know Australia,' and he was right – the entire region still conveys the strong frontier spirit on which New South Wales was founded.

TALL TALES ...

Some people claim that New South Wales's wild and violent past hasn't quite been laid to rest. The countryside is scattered with stories of strange apparitions and **restless ghosts**. Maitland Jail, where public executions were held and conditions were brutal, reportedly still echoes with the anguished cries of its long-gone inmates. The town hall of Picton, south-west of Sydney, is said to be visited by a black-coated figure as well as a ghost-child who occasionally appears on the stage. Monte Christo house, in Junee, near Wagga Wagga, is visited by about 100 ghost-hunters every year. It is said that the ghost of Mrs Crawley, the unhappy Victorian housewife who first lived in the mansion, still paces the halls.

Whip-cracking fun at the world-renowned **Tamworth Country Music Festival**.

With a vibrant community atmosphere, country New South Wales offers a social life with a difference.

A few years ago, it was all about the 'seachange'. Now, a new wave of city- and coast-dwellers is discovering the benefits of life in the country – they have been dubbed the 'treechangers'. With a vibrant community atmosphere, country New South Wales offers a social life with a difference. Think rollicking Bachelor and Spinster balls, the world-renowned Tamworth Country Music Festival and unforgettable ute musters, like the one at Deniliquin, alongside a naturally healthy lifestyle and stunning scenery.

And country towns are welcoming the new arrivals. Local councils hope that young couples and families will start new businesses such as shops, cafés and guesthouses, which will, in turn, attract the growing ranks of

LOCAL LEGENDS

No mention of the NSW country could leave out **Henry Lawson**. Born on the Grenfell goldfields, Lawson travelled the outback widely, where he drew inspiration for his evocative bush poems and sketch stories. In later life he became a beggar and a drunk and even did some jail time for non-payment of alimony. For a while he was Australia's most notorious celebrity, but when he died in 1922, he was granted a huge show of respect and an official state funeral.

grey nomads, the retirees who've sold up to travel around the country in their newly acquired caravans and motorhomes. Everyone benefits.

Country New South Wales certainly doesn't lack in the all-important cultural and cosmopolitan 'comforts'. Its foodie delights, for example, rival those of any state capital, with an increasing array of locally produced boutique wines, cheeses and organic fruits and vegetables on the menu. But these regions still offer a sense of serenity. The picturesque rolling hills and flowing rivers, seasonally changing flora and quaint, historic towns bring a welcome respite from the crowds and concrete jungles of the big cities and rapidly expanding coastal areas.

The **Deniliquin Ute Muster** is a record-breaking event, not just for its parade of utes, but also for the largest blue singlet muster.

EARTHLYDELIGHTS

The glorious produce of country New South Wales guarantees the state's inhabitants stay extremely well fed. Pockets of foodie delights crop up all over the state.

Take the south coast, for example. In quaint country towns like Berry, beautiful Devonshire teas give a nostalgic taste of our English heritage. Meanwhile, those in search of true blue fare can head to Jervis Bay, where bush-tucker tours are on offer to those who are a little more gastronomically adventurous.

Jamberoo is well known for its action theme park, but nestling in the surrounding hills is also the Elise Pascoe International Cooking School, where connoisseurs can take a cooking course or master class, depending on how much they want to impress their friends. Even further south, docile cows chew the grass off the fairytale green hills of Bega – the source of the cheese that has made the area famous.

Of course, New South Welshmen need a good drink to wash down their good food. Wollongong is home to Australia's largest micro-brewery, the Five Islands Brewing Company, but the state's favourite drink would have to be wine.

The beautiful Hunter Valley is home to lush forests and rich pastureland, and is a dedicated foodies' destination – the Lovedale Long Lunch being one of the most popular events. Its signature, however, is without doubt its international reputation as a grape-growing and wine-producing hotspot. Grape vines were first planted in the region in the 1820s, by pioneering vignerons such as George Wyndham of Dalwood, William Kelman at Kirkton and James King of Irrawang. Today, if you shut your eyes and poke a finger at a map of the region, you're certain to hit on one of the more than 120 wineries and cellar doors, famed drops such as De Bortoli, Lindemans, McGuigan and Brokenwood. Taking a self-guided tour, such as the Upper Hunter Wine Trail, which takes in vineyards from Broke to Scone, is a fail-safe and scenic way to discover the Hunter's best tipples. The region is also a world-famous cultural mecca for musicians and their festivals: whether you're after a little light jazz, opera, blues or classical – perfect with a bottle of red – it can be found in the Hunter.

Peter Darley, an apple grower in **Orange**.

Coolangatta Estate
De Bortoli
Grevillea Estate
Lindemans
McGuigan Wines
Rosemount Estate
Scarborough Wine Co.
Stone Creek
Tyrrell's Wines
Wyndham Estate

TASTE OF THE COUNTRY

Hand-made Morpeth Sourdough bread
Pukara Estate Premium Olive Oil
Oysters from Greenwell Point and Batemans Bay
Bellata Gold Pasta
Disaster Bay Chillies
Cheese from Tilba or the Bega Valley
Pecans from Trawalla and Brookfarm macadamias
Snowy Mountains Cookies
Serendipity Ice Cream
Organic treats from the Junee Liquorice & Chocolate Factory

The lounge at **Logan Wines**, Mudgee.

SPORTFILE

A race meeting at **Broken Hill**.

oday more than ever, NSW is 'the world capital of sport hobbyists', as *The Sydney Morning Herald*'s Roy Masters has described it. Its sports fans revel in choice rather than passionate commitment to a single code.

For many years rugby league was the traditional winter staple, but since the 1990s, competition for fans in the country's most populous state has become stiffer than ever, due to the coming of age of Australian Rules, rugby union and soccer.

The South Melbourne Football Club moved to NSW and became the Sydney Swans back in 1982, but it wasn't until the arrival of a man they called 'Plugger' that New South Welshmen stopped calling the game 'aerial ping pong' and making jokes about tight shorts. Tony Lockett came to Sydney to finish his career in 1995, helped the Swans to a grand final a year later and broke Gordon Coventry's all-time goal-scoring record in 1999 at the Sydney Cricket Ground. Sydney loves a winner. She climbed aboard and was rewarded when the club, under former player Paul Roos, won its first premiership in 2005 – and almost did it again a year later.

As far as NSW was concerned, rugby union was a game played by private schoolboys, lawyers and bankers until the sport went professional in 1995 and the Wallabies won the 1999 World Cup in France as well as five Bledisloe Cups from 1998 to 2002.

And soccer was played mostly by 'sheilas, wogs and poofters', according to the tongue-in-cheek title of the late great Johnny

A panoramic montage of the Doug Walters Stand at the **SCG** on Day 2 of the Fifth Test Match.

Warren's history of the game. Narrowly missing out on the World Cup finals in 1998 and 2002 didn't help soccer's chances of being taken seriously in Sydney, but when Australia beat Uruguay in a penalty shoot-out at the city's Olympic stadium to make the 2006 event, traffic was stopped in the CBD and an impromptu midnight street party erupted. Soccer had arrived. As the national A-League competition was launched, basing teams in Newcastle, Sydney and the Central Coast, the Socceroos went to Germany '06, where they were robbed – robbed, I tell you – of a quarter-finals spot by the theatrics of an Italian defender in the final seconds of their game against the eventual champions.

In summer, cricket still rules the sporting calendar, with support from basketball and the annual Sydney to Hobart yacht race, and in autumn and spring the horse racing carnivals strip sports fans of any money they've been able to save in the summer or winter.

And then there are the events where sport is just a backdrop. At the annual picnic races in Bong Bong and Orange, the horses run a distant second to the action in the off-course marquees, as about 4000 revellers pour an average of $250,000 down their throats and into the local economy.

Up close and personal with a **Sydney Swans** fan.

THESPORTINGCALENDAR

JANUARY book a seat on Yabba's Hill at the SCG and watch five days of the **Sydney Test Match** unfold, then return for the finals of the **one-day cricket series**.

FEBRUARY catch the **A-League soccer finals** and don the budgie smugglers for the 2-kilometre **Cole Classic** ocean swim at Manly.

MARCH hit the beach again for the **Surf Life Saving Championships**, then head west to Rosehill Racecourse for the **Golden Slipper**, the world's richest race for two-year-olds.

APRIL frock or suit up again for the **Autumn Racing Carnival** at Sydney's Royal Randwick.

MAY get to know Sydney's streets the hard way in the **annual half-marathon**, watch the NSW Waratahs bomb out again in the **Super 14** rugby union finals, and get behind the NSW Blues in the **State of Origin** series against Queensland.

JULY rugby gets serious with the annual **Tri-Nations series** and the big one, **the Bledisloe Cup**, against New Zealand's awesome All Blacks.

AUGUST join more than 60,000 footsoldiers in the 14-kilometre **City2Surf** fun run from Hyde Park to Bondi Beach.

SEPTEMBER it's the business end of the **AFL** and **NRL seasons**, and the Sydney Swans are usually thereabouts.

OCTOBER after the **Spring Racing carnival**, cross the Great Dividing Range for the **Bathurst 1000** touring car race.

NOVEMBER saddle up for the **Sydney to the Gong bike ride** and **Bong Bong Picnic Races** in the southern highlands.

DECEMBER round out the year by getting on the harbour and watching the start of the **Sydney to Hobart yacht race**.

The **Sydney to Hobart** yacht race, leaving the harbour.

THEGAMESWEPLAY

If the people of NSW liked to watch the same sports they like to participate in, it would be Friday-night walking with the crowds at the end of each week, not football. Or it might be Friday-night aerobics, under lights, with a bit of rockfishing at half-time.

Statistics on the participation rates of various sports prove that playing sport and watching it are two entirely different kettles of fish,

Participation rates of various sports prove that playing sport and watching it are two entirely different kettles of fish.

Surf-boat racing at Coogee Beach.

Whether you call it football or **soccer**, it's our new favourite sport.

and that enjoyable exercise doesn't necessarily make such enjoyable television. The most popular ways of keeping fit in New South Wales are walking, aerobics, swimming and cycling, in that order.

In the winter, soccer is now officially the most played football code among kids, a trend fed by the game's burgeoning popularity on the small screen and by the perception among parents that it's less dangerous than the rugby codes. In the 12 months leading up to the Australian Bureau of Statistics's last sports participation survey, four per cent of New South Welshpeople played soccer – which was more than in any other state.

Of course, generalisations about what people like to play in the state ignore the fact that one end of it is very different to the other. As you fly south from Sydney to Melbourne, the Australian Rules epidemic doesn't begin at the border town of Albury-Wodonga. Gradually, the green mown fields change from rectangles to ovals from about Canberra onwards, and now more and more are being replaced by soccer fields.

OURSPORTINGHEROES

You can tell a lot about a person by their heroes. You can tell a lot about a state, too. Would the inimitable Shane Warne be as popular in New South Wales or South Australia as he is in Victoria, where sport is a religion and the MCG its Mecca? Would it be as easy for sporting legends like former aerial skiing champion Kirstie Marshall or Aussie Rules player Justin Madden to get into politics in New South Wales? Would Wally Lewis, despite all his rugby league achievements, be The King if he had played for New South Wales instead of the perennial underdogs, Queensland?

Who, then, are NSW's current heroes and what do they tell us about the state's sports fans?

There's been no display of adulation in recent years quite like the 2003 SCG farewell for Bankstown boy Stephen Rodger Waugh, the 168-Test architect of Australian cricket's most successful era ever. But then, Waugh did reach 100 with a boundary on the last ball of the day, so some of the crowd's roaring, standing ovation must have been for the victorious way in which he said goodbye and avoided the selectors' looming axe.

The same could be said for the Dubbo-born, Narramine-raised bowler Glenn 'Pigeon' McGrath, who took a wicket with his last

Retired swim star, **Ian Thorpe** with his dogs.

Retired cricketer **Glenn McGrath**'s last ball for the Aussies during the Fifth Test of the Ashes at the SCG (Australia won the series 5–0).

Retired rugby player **Andrew Johns** scoring a try in the NRL finals

Women's surf pro **Layne Beachley** riding the waves at the Havaianas Beachley Classic.

ball in test cricket at the SCG in 2006, inspiring similar scenes of celebration. How much of the ruckus was for McGrath, whose 563 Test Match wickets were the most ever by a fast bowler, and how much was for the magic of that particular moment, which completed a 5–0 Ashes series whitewash against the old enemy England?

The results of Sydney's Ian Thorpe spoke for themselves during his eight-year reign at the top of world swimming – as did the fact that he retired at the age of 24, making every worker in the country green with envy. The 'Thorpedo' won nine Olympic Games medals including five golds, the most by any Australian ever. His 11 world championship gold medals and the six he won at Fukuoka in Japan in 2001 were also both records and he broke no fewer than 13 regulation world records. To top it off he was voted Young Australian of the Year in 2000 and remains a dedicated philanthropist and fashion pioneer.

Then there's Manly's Layne Beachley, who turned professional at the age of 16, was ranked sixth in the world by the age of 20, then beat chronic fatigue syndrome to become the best professional woman surfer ever, with seven world titles so far – and counting.

But how do you measure those statistics against the repeated performances under pressure of a team player like Andrew Johns? Often called the world's best in either rugby code, Cessnock's favourite son won man-of-the-match at his first grade debut, played for NSW and Australia in his first full season, took the Newcastle Knights to the first of two premierships – playing the grand final with three broken ribs – in year three, won the Dally M medal a record three times, and captained NSW and Australia to several series wins. When Johns played, the theory went, Newcastle, NSW and Australia won. When he didn't, it was a fair fight. With his early retirement in April 2007, everyone else can now breathe a sigh of relief.

ARTSANDCULTURE

Since a bunch of crooks and soldiers gathered in 1789 for the colony's first play, *The Recruiting Officer*, performed by a bunch of convicts near present-day Bligh Street, high and low culture have happily lived side by side in New South Wales.

It may look like a work of art in its own right, but the Sydney Opera House is first and foremost a place where other art happens. It was designed to showcase the high arts, as performed by the Sydney Symphony Orchestra, the Australian Ballet or Opera Australia, but the sails and their surrounds are just as likely in the 21st century to play host to an *Australian Idol* final, a Kerry Packer funeral or John Farnham's latest comeback tour.

At the Art Gallery of New South Wales, the most popular annual show is the Archibald Prize, a $35,000 portrait-painting competition that some purists have labelled a 'horse race' and which, in 2007, even featured its first singing portrait. The artist, Dr Peter Smeeth, painted the soprano Amelia Farrugia and strapped a CD player of her recordings to the back of the canvas.

The stately Australian Museum is the nation's foremost natural history research institution, but many of its visitors come for travelling exhibitions about body piercing and death.

The **Art Gallery of NSW**.

The **Living Desert Sculpture Park** in Broken Hill.

READ ... WATCH ... LISTEN TO ...

AB 'Banjo' Paterson 'I had written him a letter which I had, for want of better / Knowledge, sent to where I met him down the Lachlan, years ago'.

DH Lawrence's *Kangaroo* written in Thirroul, north of Wollongong, and immortalised in a painting by Australian artist Sidney Nolan.

Thomas Keneally for local colour from the multi-award-winning author, try *The Chant of Jimmie Blacksmith* (1978), based on the life of New South Wales bushranger Jimmy Governor.

The Dish the 2000 film by the creators of *The Castle* about the role of Parkes's radio antenna in the first Apollo moon landing.

The Matrix* Trilogy**, ***Superman Returns, ***Mission: Impossible: II*** all Hollywood blockbusters filmed in Sydney.

Slim Dusty he sang about the bush in 'A pub with no beer' and the city in 'I'd love to have a beer with Duncan'.

Silverchair the ever-popular Newcastle band with a consistent string of top 20 hits to their name.

A melted ice cream van sculpture at the annual **Sculpture by the Sea** art event.

Showing the links between Sydney's culture and its working class origins, the science-focused Powerhouse Museum sits in the shell of an old power station, the Sydney Theatre Company resides in what was once a bustling wharf and the Museum of Contemporary Art lives in the Maritime Services Board building. Outside the city, Tinonee's 22-seat Terrace Cinema – the world's smallest in operation – is built in an 1880 maternity hospital, while the chamber music festival at Huntington Estate is played among the barrels and bottles.

ART IN THE OPEN

Since 1997 the annual **Sculpture by the Sea** competition has attracted artists from all over the world, who construct wild and imaginative outdoor sculptures to decorate the coastal walk between the Eastern Suburbs beaches of Bondi and Tamarama. The first-place winner takes home a $30,000 prize, but one suspects the artists do it for fun more than money. Previous entries have included a giant pair of sunglasses and a school of silver-lamé fish suspended on a curtain in front of the waves.

The crowd joins in at the **Big Day Out** (above).

Outrageous fun at **Mardi Gras** (far left).

Doug Cruikshank and Cliff Smith prepare their dahlias for judging at the **Royal Easter Show** (left).

THEFESTIVALCALENDAR

The NSW substratum of the culture vulture species can spend all four seasons of the year just trying to migrate from one major event to the next. Here's a small sample:

The Sydney Festival cutting-edge world theatre, dance, visual arts and music combined with the best of Australian artists – and it makes a profit!

Australia Day Sydney's celebration means fireworks, concerts, ferry races and flags, everywhere.

The Big Day Out Australia's biggest popular music festival began in Sydney back in 1992 and now features some of the biggest bands and DJs on the planet.

The Tamworth Country Music Festival bush balladeers come together in regional NSW to compete for the Golden Guitar Awards.

Chinese New Year when Chinatown is even livelier than usual.

Tropfest the world's biggest short film festival was begun by actor/director John Polson in the Tropicana Cafe, Darlinghurst.

The Sydney Gay and Lesbian Mardi Gras the world's biggest gay pride march, which pulls a global crowd.

The Archibald Prize debate the judges' verdict, then scoff at the notion of a painting competition.

Byron Bay Blues and Roots Festival an Easter weekend tradition in the easternmost town in Australia.

Royal Easter Show the state's other, older Easter tradition, when the bush comes to the big smoke.

Sydney Writers' Festival where readers can put a face to the names of their favourite authors.

Sydney Film Festival an opportunity to escape the winter chill at screenings, debates and red carpet events.

Coffs Harbour Buskers' Festival try out your song and dance routine or simply toss a coin into someone else's hat at this annual gathering of street performers.

Homebake every December the Domain plays host to this music festival for Aussie acts only.

WHAT IN THE WEIRD?

Parkes is, for most of the year, a fairly average rural town in the Central West. But if you visited in January, you'd be forgiven for thinking it harbours an amazing secret. Yes, it's true, Elvis lives in Parkes. Well, at least, hordes of his impersonators do during the annual **Elvis Parkes Festival**. It all started in 1993, when a group of local fans – one of whom changed his name to Elvis – got together at the local restaurant, Graceland, to celebrate the King's birthday. By 2007 the festival attracted around 6000 other visitors tempted by events such as the Elvis Gospel Service, the Miss Priscilla Dinner and Big Hair competition or barefoot bowls at Elvis on the Green. A new world record was set for the most Elvises in one place: 147.

CURRENT**DARLINGS**

Ever since Peter Allen vowed 'I still call Australia home', we've loved an Aussie who does well overseas – particularly one who comes home afterwards. Even if they grew up elsewhere, stars are quickly adopted, particularly if they adopt New South Wales.

New South Wales has always adored North Shore girl Nicole Kidman – even when she married Tom Cruise – but is doubly fond of her since she found Keith Urban, the Aussie who quietly conquered Nashville. The state rejoiced at the spectacular scenes of their 2006 wedding at the Cardinal Cerrett: Chapel atop the cliffs at Manly.

And when the Oscar-winning actress Cate Blanchett announced,

Cate Blanchett, Andrew Upton and their son march for Global Climate Justice.

in 2006, that she would be taking over the running of the Sydney Theatre Company with her director husband Andrew Upton, the high-brow *New Yorker* magazine said it was the first time a movie star of Cate's standing had given so much back to the theatre scene that had launched her career. In Australia, too, Blanchett's decision to spend more time at home won her many fans. She wanted her kids to grow up down under, she said, and who wouldn't?

People still aren't sure whether they love Russell Crowe, but they approve of the fact that he lives in Sydney, and that he loves rugby league so much that he bought half of his beloved South Sydney Rabbitohs club.

We all love an Aussie who does well overseas, particularly one who comes home afterwards.

Welsh-born artist John Beard is another who was officially welcomed by the Sydney establishment when he won the 2007 Archibald Prize. Of course, not everyone agreed with the result – they never do. But, as Paul Keating once said, 'What other country in the world has an annual barney over a portrait prize?'

NSW is also the base for some of the nation's most innovative artists working in the world's oldest continuous culture. The Bangarra Dance Theatre takes its name from the Wiradjeri for 'to make fire' and aims to energise the link between indigenous cultures and contemporary artistic expression. In this, the company is succeeding, winning critical acclaim in Australia and all over the world.

Archibald Prize winner John Beard with his subject, Janet Laurence.

Dancer Patrick Thaiday in the **Bangarra Dance Theatre** work 'Boomerang'.

NATURAL WONDERS

The varied and wild country of New South Wales has been the source of many Dreamtime legends and the inspiration for generations of bush poets. Its natural wonders are beautiful and diverse – both living and non-living, on land and on sea, above the ground and below, ancient and always changing.

The Three Sisters in the Blue Mountains World Heritage Area is perhaps the state's most famous natural landmark. Known individually as Meehni, Wimlah and Gunnedoo, Aboriginal legend has it that the sisters were turned to stone by a witch-doctor who died before he could turn them back into people again.

The best way to see the whole area, with its precipitous, bush-carpeted valleys and eroded sandstone peaks, is slowly. This can be achieved by taking three days to walk the 45-kilometre 'Six Foot Track'. Named for its width, the track takes you from the Explorers' Tree near Katoomba to another of the state's wonders, the Jenolan Caves, one of the oldest cave systems in the world.

Further north is Lake Macquarie, an inland sea twice the size of Sydney Harbour, and the World Heritage-listed Barrington Tops National Park. Spread across 120,000 hectares of wilderness, Barrington Tops provides shelter to more than 26 animal species, many of which are endangered.

The Far North Coast Hinterland boasts incredible rainforests, many of which have been carefully protected from logging. These sub-tropical remnants of an ancient volcanic world are abundant in weird and wonderful wildlife, like the bent-winged bat and wompoo fruit dove, which make their home in Nightcap National Park, part of the World Heritage-listed Central Eastern Rainforest.

The famous **Three Sisters** in the beautiful Blue Mountains.

Snow-capped mountains in **Kosciuszko** National Park

FIVE OF THE BEST ... **NATIONAL PARKS**

Dorrigo this World Heritage-listed park offers a beguiling view from its elevated 'skywalk' above the rainforest canopy.

Kosciuszko centring around Australia's highest peak, this alpine wonderland in the Snowy Mountains is popular with skiers in winter and hikers in the warmer months.

Mount Warning forming part of a large extinct volcano, the mountain was named because the first explorers used it as a landmark that signified offshore reefs.

Mungo World Heritage-listed for the incredible archaeological finds discovered here, the park is also famous for its 33 km-long rock formation, the Walls of China.

Warrumbungle home to strangely magnificent rock formations, including the eye-catching Bread Knife, the park also offers views beyond our world at the Sliding Spring Observatory, the largest astronomy research facility in Australia.

A serene mist drops over the **Hawkesbury River**.

Down south, the land reveals its age at the Pinnacles of Ben Boyd National Park. This colourful rock formation is around 65 million years old. The park also features a long-distance walking track, the Light to Light trail, which takes trekkers from Green Cape Lighthouse to Boyd's Tower.

New South Wales also contains Australia's oldest evidence of pre-European settlement, at the Mungo National Park, where archaeologists have uncovered human remains from 40,000 years ago. Living relics are in evidence at the wetlands area of Albury-Wodonga where iconic 700-year-old river red gums line the banks of the Murray River.

The state is also home to several marine reserves, including the gorgeous Montague Island, 8 kilometres off the coast of Narooma. It is a mini-Eden of wildlife, with the title of cutest animal hotly contested between the fur seals and the little penguins. Fifteen species of birds also breed on the tiny island, and dolphins, humpback whales and southern right whales are habitually spotted in the surrounding waters.

Even further off the coast, around 600 kilometres east of Port Macquarie, is the Lord Howe Island group. Added to the World Heritage list in 1982, these spectacular volcanic islands boast a unique biodiversity. Of the 241 species of native plants, 105 are endemic to the islands. About 168 species of seabirds nest on the islands, and many of these, such as the woodhen and providence petrel, are rare or endangered. The sparkling, crystal-clear waters around Lord Howe contain an unusual mix of temperate and tropical organisms and shelter the world's south-ernmost coral reef.

Balls Pyramid, **Lord Howe Island**.

CRIKEY!
Many Sydneysiders would be afraid to leave their shoes outside at night. This may be because they're soft city folk, but it's also because the state is home to one of the world's deadliest spiders. The Sydney **funnel-web** is a large, aggressive, black spider with enormous fangs. Its venom is highly toxic and can cause twitching, vomiting and even heart failure. The good news is that there is an antivenene.

LOCAL LEGENDS

In years gone by, **whale hunters** were a regular sight on the New South Wales coast, but the humans would sometimes get help from an unlikely source. Around the waters of Eden, a pod of killer whales was known to herd baleen whales into the bay and towards the harpoons of waiting whalers. The mercenary killer whales would advertise their presence by thrashing around in the sea, and in return for their 'catch' would receive the tongue of their prey. The most famous of their group, Old Tom, was sometimes said to jump on top of a harpooned whale's blow-hole to hasten its death, or even to tow boats for fun. When Old Tom died in 1930, his skeleton was preserved and is now displayed at the Eden Killer Whale Museum.

Trees reflected in the **Bournda Lagoon**.

The **National Carillon** was a gift from Britain to celebrate the 50th birthday of the capital. It contains 53 bronze bells.

AUSTRALIAN INSTITUTE OF SPORT

Founded in 1981 after the severe embarrassment of the 1976 Montreal Olympic Games, in which Australia failed to win a single gold medal, the Institute's well-funded programs are credited with creating Australia's success on the world sporting stage.

At the **Australian War Memorial** (above), visitors can add poppies to the bronze plaque honouring our war dead.

The Basketballer (left), created by Dominique Sutton, was commissioned to celebrate the 2000 Paralympic Games and now resides at the Australian Institute of Sport.

CAPITALDINING

In the past, people have been rather unkind about Canberra, depicting it as an unsophisticated, frumpy sort of place. Percy Deane, secretary to the Prime Minister's department under Billy Hughes, said the best view of Canberra was 'from the back of a departing train,' and Elspeth Huxley, sister of Aldous Huxley, described it disdainfully as the most middle-class city in the world.

Of course, neither of those two lived to see it flourish into the foodies' paradise it has become today. Nestled as it is in farmland and bush, the quality of produce in Canberra's restaurants and cafés is excellent, and the well-planned boulevards allow pleasant open-air dining.

The streets of Manuka, lined with boutiques and trinket shops, are the home of Canberra's café society. A constantly busy favourite is Caph's or, for a slightly more upmarket choice, there's The Tryst, which offers modern Australian cuisine at mid-range prices. For something more exotic, there's Mecca Bah Manuka, a Moroccan restaurant with floor-cushion seating and low, lantern lighting.

Kingston also has excellent eat streets, with Zest Café and the Holy Grail being a couple of the local favourites. The suburb is also the home of several British-style pubs, which bring its main square alive at night.

The Hippo Lounge in Civic shows that Canberra does do cool. With its dark wood, red walls and red ottomans, it's the perfect venue for the jazz bands that play there. The cocktail list only adds to the appeal. The Phoenix Bar is another hip drinking joint, and is a big favourite with live bands. If anyone's hungry after all that drinking, the Chairman and Yip in Civic does excellent modern Chinese cuisine. The Boathouse, set on Lake Burley Griffin, lays claim to one of the best views in Canberra, although the title would be hotly contested by Water's Edge, a classy café with panoramic vistas.

Canberra's most elegant eating experience comes in the form of afternoon tea at the Hyatt, a luxurious Art Deco hotel which serves up a dose of old world glamour along with its very fine scones.

Serious drinking is to be had at the **Wig & Pen**. It has ten different beers brewed on the premises.

At **The Ginger Room** in Old Parliament House, lush, country fare is the speciality with choices such as roasted spatchcock with saffron polenta or silverbeet strudel with asparagus sauce.

MARKET FRESH

Surrounded by fertile farmland, Canberrans have access to a wide array of fresh produce. **Canberra Region Farmers' Market** is the largest regional market in the Southern Tablelands. Held every Saturday morning in the Kuringai Building in Exhibition Park, its bustling stalls sell organic fruit and vegetables, fowls and oysters, pickles and cakes, wools and soaps, meat and cheese. On the first Sunday of every month, the **Hall Markets** attract stallholders from as far afield as Victoria and Queensland, and punters can buy everything from fresh fruit and vegetables to worm farms and puppies. But for Canberra's true gourmands, **Belconnen Fresh Food Markets** are number one. Thirty-one stores offer a selection of fine foods, from organic meats to speciality cheeses and antipasto. The markets even house their own cooking school, Cooking Co-ordinates.

FRESHAIRANDSUNSHINE

From well-groomed parks and gardens to tangled bushland, Canberrans have a lot of outdoors space to choose from, and they tend to spend a lot of their time there.

Canberra is known for its sharp turning of seasons. Come autumn its streets are spotted rusty-gold with falling leaves, and in winter the crisp air is complemented by clear, sunny skies, which often promise the whiff of snow from the nearby ski fields. Spring brings Floriade – a world-famous flower festival which brightens up Canberra with its 12,700 square metres of flower beds. Over 700,000 bulbs and 684,000 annuals colour the exhibition, which attracts 300,000 visitors a year. Despite being the number one tourist drawcard to the territory, entry to the festival remains free.

In the city itself, life revolves around Lake Burley Griffin – Canberra's approximate geographic centre. A jog or cycle along the shores of this artificial lake is punctuated with landmarks such as the water jet of the Captain Cook Memorial or the bell tower of the National Carillon.

For those looking to escape city streets, 30 minutes drive can bring you to nature reserves and national parkland. Almost half of the territory is actually part of Namadgi National Park in the west and south-west. It is here that many Canberrans go to bushwalk or mountain bike. The territory's Aboriginal heritage can be seen at sites such as the Birrigai rockshelter, which contains evidence that humans lived here around 21,000 years ago. More recent history was made at the nearby space tracking station at Honeysuckle Creek – the first place on earth to receive the famous images of Neil Armstrong walking on the moon.

The Cotter River, which snakes through the Namadgi National Park, provides fresh water to Canberra, but is also a popular recreation spot for family picnics and barbeques. The Cotter Route, which was badly affected by the 2003 bushfires, is a scenic 1.6-kilometre drive that winds from the city centre through the Narrabundah Hill Pine Plantation, past Casuarina Sands and into the Cotter Avenue river area.

FIVE OF THE BEST ...
OUTDOOR ACTIVITIES

Air sports kiting, flying, ballooning, hang-gliding – all are available in the ACT.

Cycling the city's network of paths is a cyclist's dream, while rougher trails can be negotiated in Namadgi National Park.

Fishing carp, redfin perch and rainbow trout all make Lake Burley Griffin their home.

Rowing whether for a leisurely paddle or a strenuous row, Lake Burley Griffin is the place for water-based fun.

Walking the territory has the full range of walks, from gentle strolls in the park to long-distance trails – the 650 km Australian Alps Walking Track starts/finishes in Namadgi National Park.

A rower (top) crosses **Lake Burley Griffin** at sunset. The city's ample stretches of water make this a popular pastime.

Junior rangers (above) come to grips with echidnas and other native wildlife at **Booderee Botanic Gardens**.

In the breathtaking **Brindabella Valley** (main picture), early morning mist rolls across farmland reminiscent of a Fred McCubbin painting.

ARTSANDCULTURE

Canberra is home to some of the nation's most important museums, galleries and cultural institutions, reflecting Australia's history, culture and way of life. It also hosts an array of eclectic festivals from the Arabian Horse Society Marathon to the Fireside Festival or the Days of Wine and Roses.

The National Museum of Australia explores the key issues, people and events that have shaped Australia. It has five permanent exhibitions which feature state-of-the-art technology displays and interactive exhibits. The National Library is also worth a look, although with three million books and an ever-growing collection on Australiana, visitors may have to go back several times to really appreciate it.

Other crowd pleasers are Questacon (the National Science and Technology Centre) – with hands-on exhibits that explain scientific phenomena better than your teacher ever did – and the National Gallery. Located next to the High Court, the gallery is home to some of the country's best art pieces – from Jackson Pollock's 'Blue Poles' to the works of home-grown artists such as Tom Roberts and Arthur Streeton. Sidney Nolan's 'Ned Kelly' is also part of the collection.

Jackson Pollock's **Blue Poles** was a controversial purchase in 1973, but has dramatically increased in value and remains one of the National Gallery's most popular exhibits.

Other recognisable faces are found at the National Portrait Gallery. Its standing collection features prominent Australians who have made a contribution to their particular field of endeavour. Recent acquisitions include a portrait of actor Alex Dimitriades by Michael Zavros and a portrait of musician Nick Cave by Ashley Mackevicius.

Canberra's theatre and performance hub is the Canberra Theatre Centre, which hosts travelling ballet companies, orchestras and theatre groups. The Australian Ballet and the Bell Shakespeare Company are regular visitors.

A more family-friendly ACT festival is Celebrate Canberra, which is held annually in March. It involves a theatre and dance program and outdoor sports demonstrations, all aimed at bringing attention to the region. Canberra also hosts the National Folk Festival, which attracts thousands of people from all over Australia, to listen to folk acts like Cloudstreet, Alistair Hulett and Dick Gaughan. Every night during the festival there is a grand dance, starting with a Scottish Ball and culminating in an Australian colonial ball. And if you're here in winter, there's nothing better to beat the blues than the Fireside Festival, tasting regional food and wine by the side of a roaring fire.

The **Balloon Fiesta** (above), flying high for over 23 years.

The glorious bulbs of **Floriade** are complemented by art exhibits and a popular gnome decorating competition.

If you love the smell of burning rubber, Canberra offers **SummerNats**, Australia's best known car carnival. Held annually in January, SummerNats attracts revheads from far and wide, and is estimated to bring about $12 million to the ACT's economy. Prizes are given out for the best burnouts and a Miss SummerNats is appointed every year.

Heart Reef in the Whitsundays, Great Barrier Reef.

QUEENSLAND

'Beautiful one day, perfect the next.' To outsiders,
advertising slogans sum up the Sunshine State – all
beaches, rainforests, resorts and theme parks. Even
the banana benders pride themselves on living life
at a holiday pace. But like a lush tropical plant,
Queensland is growing fast and furiously.

STATEFILE

The first people to make this area home were the Aboriginal people who migrated across the Torres Strait by boat or land bridge some 40,000 or more years ago. The 17th century brought more overseas visitors, including Captain James Cook and Matthew Flinders, but the Great Barrier Reef presented a huge danger for ships and made inland exploration difficult.

In 1823 John Oxley sailed north from Sydney, looking for sites to form another penal settlement, and found the Brisbane River at Moreton Bay. A year later he established a permanent colony here, and it was earmarked for the more intractable convicts. Not long after this, in 1839, the transportation of convicts to Australia ceased, and the Brisbane colony was closed, but the population started to expand again when free settlement began in 1842.

Over the next decade a sense of identity began to grow among the settlers here, as they realised the importance of Brisbane as a port, linked by land with the northern pastoral settlements and by sea with ports of Sydney and London. The settlement's remoteness from the administrative centre of Sydney also caused tensions, and added to the feeling that independence was the only way forward. In 1851 a public meeting was held to consider separation from New South Wales, and in 1859 Queen Victoria signed the proclamation that gave Queensland separate colony status with its own governor and legislature. Unsurprisingly, the Queen vetoed the state's other suggested name, Cooksland. The state's first elections were held a year later, and Robert George Wyndham Herbert became its first premier.

A page from *The Illustrated Sydney News* in 1888, showing **Brisbane**.

Just like other states, Queensland had its own, albeit small, gold rush in the latter half of the 19th century, when gold was discovered at Canoona in 1858. Chinese settlers began to arrive in droves, and by 1877 there were 17,000 on the state's goldfields, prompting the government to place restrictions on Chinese immigration.

In 1891, the Great Shearers' Strike in Barcaldine, over the issue of employment of non-union labour, led to the establishment of the first Australian Labor Party. Fittingly, in 1899, Queenslanders elected the first Labor government in the world, even though it only lasted one week.

In more recent times, Eddie Mabo, a Torres Strait Islander, brought Queensland to worldwide notice when he began a landmark legal action in 1982 to claim ownership of his land in the Torres Strait. It led to an historic High Court decision ten years later, which recognised native title and retracted the doctrine of terra nullius, which had allowed the early colonialists to seize what they considered to be 'no one's land'.

VITAL STATISITICS

NICKNAMES: the Sunshine State, the Smart State

AREA: 1,852,642 km² (2nd)

POPULATION: 4,070,400 (3rd)

POPULATION DENSITY: 2.35 per km² (5th)

LANDMARKS: Big Pineapple, Daintree Rainforest, Treasury Casino, Whitsunday Islands

MAIN INDUSTRIES: agriculture (tropical fruit, cotton, sugar cane, cattle and wool), mining (bauxite, coal and copper) and tourism

SPORTS: rugby union, rugby league, cricket, soccer, basketball, swimming

NATIONAL PARKS: 215 including Carnarvon, Undara Volcanic, Springbrook, Simpson Desert

WORLD HERITAGE SITES: Central Eastern Rainforest Reserves, Great Barrier Reef, Fraser Island, Wet Tropics of Queensland

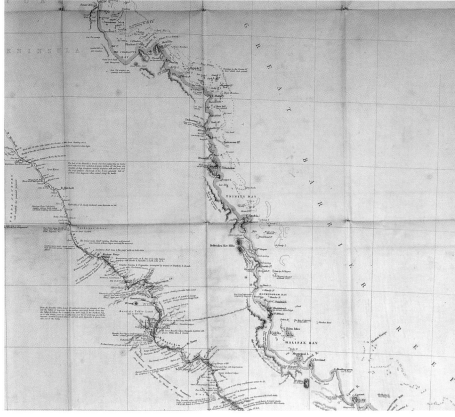

John Arrowsmith, who was known for his exquisite and elaborate maps, published this one of the **Queensland coastline** (above) in 1847.

A steam train hauling **sugar cane** (left) on the River Estate in the Mackay region around 1875.

QUEENSLAND TODAY

Queensland is a state on the move; it is the fastest growing state in Australia, with over 1500 people moving there each week, both from overseas and interstate. Predictions show it will be Australia's second most populous state, behind NSW, by the late 2020s.

It's little wonder so many people are attracted to the Sunshine State – not only does it boast stunning natural beauty and a relaxed lifestyle, but it also has great economic opportunities.

Primary industries include bananas, pineapples, peanuts, a wide variety of other tropical and temperate fruit and vegetables, grain crops, wineries, cattle raising, cotton, sugar cane, wool and a mining industry including bauxite, coal and copper.

And the boom in the tourism and mining industries over the last 20 years, as well as an expanding aerospace sector, mean the state will remain Australia's fastest growing economy into the foreseeable future. In addition, it's a cheap place to live. In 2003 Brisbane was found to have the lowest cost of living of all of Australia's capitals.

Queenslanders have a reputation for being laid-back and for liking their space, so it's no surprise that the state's population is so spread out. About 45 per cent of Queenslanders live in the state's capital, Brisbane, and the rest are spread around the country towns and outback, whereas in most of the other Australian states, the capital cities soak up an average of 63 per cent of the population.

More than anything, it's a fun place to be. The huge tourism industry, which contributes about $6 billion annually to state revenues, means new people are always passing through, and if the natural wonders aren't enough, locals can always amuse themselves at theme parks like Dreamworld, Movie World and Sea World on the Gold Coast.

With balmy weather, beautiful beaches, lush scenery, money rolling in and friendly people, Queensland today has pretty much everything going for it.

Lady Musgrave Island is an uninhabited coral cay on the Great Barrier Reef. Its aquamarine waters offer spectacular snorkelling.

SIGNS OF GOVERNMENT

Parliament House in Brisbane is by the impressive Botanic Gardens. Queensland was the first place in the world to give daily uncensored reports of debates.

Queensland's **coat of arms** displays its primary industries: wheat, sugar cane, beef, wool and gold.

The state's badge features on the **flag**, showing a Royal Crown on a Maltese Cross.

NATURAL AMBASSADORS

Cooktown orchids grow on trees and rocks in the state's tropical north. The **Barrier Reef anemone fish** was chosen as a fitting marine emblem in 2005. The **koala** was chosen as a state emblem by popular demand. Queensland's bird is the **brolga**.

PEOPLEFILE

Queenslanders are people who know how to take it easy. Their laconic humour and slow way of talking may be mocked by other states, but are probably just a natural reaction to their splendid and notoriously steamy environment. When it's that hot, and the world around you is that beautiful, why rush things?

Queenslanders live in a paradisical state, drenched in sunshine, blessed with an abundance of tropical rain, warm seas and an incredible coastline, so it's probably not surprising that they're a little bit smug about it.

They also don't like interference from outsiders. The fierce, independent spirit that led to Queensland's accession from New South Wales in 1859 can be seen in the strong political characters the state has produced, from the union men who founded Australia's first Labor party, to the controversial political figures of Sir Joh Bjelke-Petersen and Pauline Hanson.

For the most part, though, true Queenslanders don't worry too much about politics – or about anything much at all. They're too busy sipping beer on the porches of their Queenslander houses, watching the sunrise over the reef, or swinging in a hammock by the edge of a cane field.

MOST LIKELY TO SAY:

Take it easy, mate.

I wouldn't be dead for quids.

Bundy and Coke, anyone?

LEAST LIKELY TO SAY:

I think it's too early for a beer.

A bit nippy today, isn't it?

Hurry up, we don't have all day!

The notorious **Animal Bar** in Karumba is the haunt of trawler crews and jackeroos.

FLYING DOCTOR SERVICE OF AUSTRALIA QUEE...

Flight nurse Jenny Ward and Captain Ralph Teo of the **Royal Flying Doctor Service** in Cairns.

Queenslanders may be known for their easygoing style, but that hasn't stopped them from achieving success in every arena – from sport and aviation to politics and activism.

Charles Kingsford Smith was just a boy from Brisbane before he completed the first trans-Pacific flight in 1928. Another pioneer was William Lane, who helped to found the Australian Labor Movement. Although born in Bristol, he moved to Brisbane in 1885 and began writing about the plight of the working man. In 1893 he led a valiant but ultimately unsuccessful attempt to create a socialist utopia in the jungles of South America.

Queenslanders are sometimes teased for being a little slow, but their academic achievements suggest otherwise. Engineer John Bradfield, of Sydney Harbour Bridge fame, was a Queenslander. The University of Queensland produced writers Margo Kingston, Thea Astley and David Malouf, and the university also boasts Professor Ian Frazer, who became Australian of the Year in 2006 for his role in developing a vaccine for cervical cancer.

COLOURFUL CHARACTERS

Burke and Wills immortalised in Australia for their ill-fated expedition across uncharted land from Melbourne to the Gulf of Carpentaria and back in 1860–61, Robert O'Hara Burke and William John Wills were perhaps lucky to get as far as they did. Neither was experienced in exploration, and Burke (the leader) had no bush skills whatsoever. Bad luck and bad leadership plagued the party. They took a massive amount of equipment (about 20 tonnes, including a Chinese gong), but most of it had to be abandoned. On their return journey, they missed a waiting supplies team by only nine hours, then left the designated spot without leaving instructions as to their next move, which meant rescue parties couldn't find them. This spot, at Coopers Creek in south-west Queensland, is marked by a coolibah tree (now known as The Dig Tree), and is a popular destination for tourists. Burke and Wills both died near it, possibly from beri-beri, after existing for months on the Aboriginal staple of ngardu seeds.

CITYSTYLE

S ituated on the Brisbane River between the Pacific Ocean and the Great Dividing Range, some people have described Brisbane as 'a big country town', and the 1.8 million inhabitants of Australia's third largest city will tell you that that's part of its charm.

Early planning laws decreed that there should be a minimum size for residential blocks in Brisbane, meaning few terrace houses were built in the 19th century. Instead, variations on the roomy wooden Queenslander home sprang up, ensuring the Sunshine State's breezy way of life would be upheld in its capital. But now, as the country's fastest growing city – its population has doubled in the last five years – Brisbane is a city torn between its past and its future, between its signature laid-back style and its desire to get ahead, fast.

'Brisvegas' is a young city in many ways. Its people have a median age of just 32 and many of its original wooden buildings were burned down in an 1864 fire. Only two buildings remain from the early settlement: the Old Windmill, sometimes known as Observatory Tower, and the Old Commissariat Store, which was built by convicts

A city torn between its past and its future, between its signature laid-back style and its desire to get ahead, fast

when Brisbane was a penal colony and now houses the Royal Historical Society of Queensland.

But plenty of new landmarks have sprung up since. MacArthur Chambers, for example, became the headquarters of General Douglas MacArthur, Commander-in-Chief of the south-west Pacific area during World War II. And the Story Bridge, designed by John Bradfield who also engineered that bridge in Sydney, boasts some of the deepest foundations in the world at a little over 40 metres. It needs them – it's built on sand.

Brisbane is also a green city, dotted with almost 200 parks. They range from Mount Coot-tha Reserve, covering 1142 hectares and offering spectacular views of the city and Moreton Bay, to small city parks and the lush, sub-tropical City Botanic Gardens, which adorn the banks of the Brisbane River and overflow with jacarandas, frangipanis, orchids, oleanders, flame trees and bougainvilleas.

The city sprawls out from the **Brisbane River** (main picture), which is lined with gardens, cafés and parks.

Swimmers at **Streets Beach** (above right) watching the Ashes.

Bougainvillea plants adorn the arbour at **South Bank Parklands** (right).

The majestic **Conrad Treasury Casino** (main picture) oozes money.

Sashimi from Sono at Portside Wharf (below) displays Queensland's fresh produce.

Up here, they do it on Fridays.

EATSTREETS, SHOPSTREETS

As its bigger southern cousins Sydney and Melbourne bicker over which is better, smarter, more beautiful or richer, Brisbane puts its feet up and laughs off the comparisons. In a state where no one doubts that they live in paradise, the capital city doesn't see the need to enter into debate.

Its greatest asset – a sub-tropical climate – makes it a great place to eat for two reasons: you can almost always do so outdoors, and the food is fresh, abundant and delicious.

'The al fresco dining capital of Australia', as the brochures call it, has undergone a gastronomic growth spurt since the late-1980s, driven by the 1988 World's Fair (Expo) and Queensland's economic boom. The seafood, fruit and vegetables available in this part of the country were always a bit bigger, fresher and brighter than elsewhere. Now it has the culinary culture to make the most of its raw materials.

At the Treasury Casino, the Marco Polo restaurant's signature dish is Peking duck, warm shallot pancakes and hoisin sauce. At the foot of the Story Bridge, the East End area now boasts acclaimed eateries such as E'cco Bistro, Lat 27 and Circa. And at West End, on the southern side of the city, Mondo was the country's first licensed organic restaurant, while Cumquats served only native produce well before Sydney's Danks Street Depot did it down south in 2007.

The city's shopping streets are often alongside its eat streets, or one and the same. Queen Street in the city centre is the place to find all the big name stores. The Queen Adelaide Building houses all the high street names, or you can go designer at Wayne Cooper, Lisa Ho and Carla Zampatti in the Wintergarden. The Valley is the place for fresh and funky, with urban styles at Ultra Suite, Blonde Venus and Lucid Laundry. Come on a weekend to spot emerging designers at the Valley Markets or adorn yourself with gorgeous jewellery and accessories.

Just as the state avoids daylight saving, Brisbane doesn't do Thursday late-night shopping. Up here, they do it on Fridays.

BEACHLIVING

They don't call it the Sunshine State for nothing. Queensland's tropical climate and captivating natural beauty have long made it a destination for holidaymakers and retirees from other states. People now come from all over the world to feel Queensland sand between their toes.

The names alone are iconic: the Whitsundays, Cape Tribulation, Noosa ... Self-respecting surfers everywhere have heard of Kirra, Burleigh Heads and Surfers Paradise. The film *Coolangatta Gold,* starring a young Colin Friels, is one of the classics of Aussie cinema.

The Whitsunday Islands are synonymous with lazy days of sailing, diving, snorkelling or simply basking in the sunshine. The dazzling white sands of Whitehaven regularly make it into countdowns of the world's most beautiful beaches. Made up of fine grains of silica, the sand has been tested at 99.89 per cent pure.

Fraser Island, in contrast, is a place where you get to feel the sand between your tyre treads. Tourists come to test out their four-wheel-driving skills, while locals come to fish or to enjoy watching the tourists get stuck in the soft stuff.

Back on the mainland, beautiful Mission Beach – now a thriving traveller town – is flanked by World Heritage rainforest on one side and the World Heritage Barrier Reef on the other. Further north, Port Douglas is a more upmarket destination, where the rich and famous moor their yachts and dine in the divine seafood restaurants.

The great irony of Queensland beaches is, of course, that you can't swim there in summer. Unless you stay within a net or wear an attractive all-over body stocking, you risk rubbing shoulders with the deadly irukandji or box jellyfish that haunt these waters. Oh, and there are also the saltwater crocs ...

Lazy days of sailing, diving, snorkelling or simply basking in the sunshine.

Dickson's Inlet in **Port Douglas** provides a tranquil setting for the Marina Mirage shopping and restaurant complex (main picture).

Footprints in the sand at **Surfers Paradise** (inset).

GOLDCOASTGLITZ

Queenslanders may be easygoing, but there's a wilder side to the Sunshine State. On the fun-loving Gold Coast, the rule is: just flaunt it – whether you've got it or not.

Surfers Paradise is the home of true blue glam. Popularised by board-riders attracted to its long, wide beaches and legendary breaks, it's now Australia's fifth largest city, comprising sprawling shopping malls, flash hotels and casinos, a glut of eateries and drinking holes, and high-rise accommodation as far as the eye can see.

The city's distinctive skyline grew out of the relaxation of building controls in the 1950s. Over the next few decades, money poured into the area. By the 'greed is good' 1980s, barefoot surfers were almost outnumbered by the so-called 'White Shoe Brigade' of businessmen, property developers and real estate agents. It came as no surprise then to see the Q1 tower emerge from these money-rich grounds. Completed in 2005, it consists of 80 storeys and reaches a height of 323 metres – one metre less than the Eiffel Tower – making it currently the world's tallest residential building. Residents of Melbourne's Eureka Tower might protest, but Q1 beats Eureka on a little technicality.

The Gold Coast, however, is primarily about fun. It's where you'll find Australia's highest concentration of theme parks, such as Dreamworld, Sea World, Wet 'n' Wild and Warner Bros Movie World. And for older kids, there's Schoolies Week. The annual invasion of hormones, P-plates and mobile phones is a great opportunity for high school graduates from Victoria, New South Wales and Queensland to gather in the mall on Cavill Avenue and to learn all about the workings of the local constabulary.

School's out for summer, and teenagers descend on the Gold Coast for its infamous **Schoolies Week**.

On the fun-loving Gold Coast, the rule is: just flaunt it – whether you've got it or not.

When the sun goes down, **Surfers Paradise** comes into its own.

LOCAL LEGENDS

The Surfers Paradise **meter maids** were introduced in 1965 as the council's answer to the unpopularity of parking meters installed the previous year. Rather than ticket cars that have run out of time, the gold bikini-clad girls pop a few extra coins in the meter for you. With the possibility that the council may install a meter-less parking system, there is talk that the meter maids' future may be in jeopardy. They may be saved, however, by the fact that they are such a popular tourist attraction as well as valued promoters of local businesses.

If brashness and bling aren't your thing, there are more refined forms of escapism to be found in Queensland. Those who prefer their cash *sans* flash can be found spending it in some of the state's more discerning resorts – about $8 billion of it each year, to be precise!

Noosa may have been named after the Aboriginal word for' 'shady place', but it now has a shining reputation as one of the most sophisticated holiday strips in Australia. Often branded the Toorak or Double Bay of the Sunshine Coast, it's where the glitterati come to display the hours of work they've put in over the year with their teams of personal trainers, pedicurists and bikini waxers.

Away from the ostentation of Noosa, *the* destination for cashed-up visitors is a luxury eco-resort. The new buzz-word in travel, the eco-resort is a haven for individuals requiring rejuvenation from the rainforest surrounds, pampering spa treatments, organic meals and endless serenity. The top tropical resorts and spas include the Daintree Eco Lodge and Spa, Camp Eden, and the latest, Qualia.

Although Queensland doesn't have the slew of white-table-cloth eateries that its southern neighbour has, fine dining is still a delight, with Berardo's at Noosa getting gongs for regional food, and the Gold Coast's Absynthe or Brisbane's Restaurant II the other contenders.

Forget all your cares in the **Rejuvenation Spa** (main picture) at Daydream Island Resort.

Fraser Island (right) isn't just one big sand dune; it has its share of luxury.

DID YOU KNOW?

Like the most exquisitely applied make-up, **Noosa's stylish façade** can sometimes slide a little in the heat. The town is not immune to the occasional display of tackiness. After the Nambour-born record producer and songwriter Mike Chapman penned 'Simply the Best' for rock star Tina Turner, he built the three-bedroom penthouse Starlight Suite on Noosa's beachfront. If you press the button near the suite's entrance, the sound of Turner belting out 'Oooooh, you're the best' fills the apartment. You can rent it for about $2000 a night.

COUNTRYSTYLE

R ural Queensland is seductive; there's no other way to describe it. From the deep greens of tropical fruit plantations to the rich red interior to the slow, beguiling townships, it's difficult not to fall in love with it.

Banana grower Mark Spagnolo happily brings in the harvest after the previous year's cyclone.

The heat and humidity have been known to drive locals a little barmy – the average daily temperature in Cairns hovers around 30 degrees Celsius, while humidity averages around 62 per cent – so life is conducted at a very relaxed pace. And this hot-house climate is great for the farmers; things just grow and grow.

The high plateau of the Atherton Tablelands, south-west of Cairns, was originally a tin-mining area, but soon became prized for its 'red gold' – the red cedar of the rainforest. Around the turn of the 20th century, Chinese immigrants drifted into the area from the Palmer River Goldfields. Here they established dairy farms, which still form the basis of the region's economy, alongside sugar cane, corn, avocados, strawberries, macadamia nuts, mangoes and citrus.

Queensland produces around 95 per cent of Australia's sugar cane. The town of Bundaberg serves a number of local plantations and mills but is perhaps more famous for its eponymous rum. US troops who came here for recreation during World War II liked mixing their rum with Cola, inspiring the Bundaberg Rum company in 1942 to begin selling it in premixed bottles. Today the town is a popular destination for backpackers looking for agricultural work, recreation and rum.

This is true Waltzing Matilda country.

LOCAL LEGENDS

Jackie Howe on 10 October, 1892, shearer Jack Howe shot to fame when he shore 321 sheep in seven hours and 40 minutes using hand shears – that's one sheep every 86 seconds. It took 58 years before anyone could do better using mechanical shears.

Howe's name also lives on as a term for the quintessential shearer's item of clothing. Shearers traditionally wore long-sleeved flannel shirts, but Jackie's wife Victoria cut off his sleeves to give him greater freedom of movement. Others copied, creating the Jackie Howe singlet.

Captain Starlight in 1870, Harry Redford and two accomplices stole 1000 head of cattle and drove them 2400 kilometres from Bowen Downs to South Australia, where they were sold. Redford's adventurous journey opened up a new southern stock trade route, and when he was finally brought to trial in 1873, he was found 'not guilty' by an adoring jury. He was later dubbed 'Captain Starlight' in a classic Australian novel, *Robbery Under Arms*, by Rolf Boldrewood. His most famous legacy in the Longreach district is the hill Starlight's Lookout, also known as Cassidy's Knob, where Redford reportedly placed a man to keep watch while he gathered the cattle for his epic journey.

WHAT IN THE WEIRD?

Boulia Camel Races every year in July the small town of Boulia in western Queensland hosts the Melbourne Cup of camel racing. With $30,000 up for grabs, the racers and trainers take the competition very seriously.

Outback Muster and Drovers' Reunion held annually at the Australian Stockman's Hall of Fame, this is a weekend of campfire storytelling, damper-making, billy-boiling and boot throwing, to pay tribute to the outback workers, drovers, stockmen, jackaroos and jillaroos who work Australia's valuable stock routes.

The Gympie Gold Rush Festival this festival's highlight is the Gold Panning Championships, when contestants are given a 15-kilogram bucket of washed gravel with gold flakes in it. Points are given for each piece of gold found. Contestants get to keep all the gold they find.

Timing and teamwork are key: **steer wrestling** at the Marburg Rodeo.

SPORTFILE

As the Brisbane-born journalist Hugh Lunn famously said when lobbying the QRL head Ron McAuliffe for the now annual State of Origin rugby series to be initiated in 1980, 'there is no such thing as an ex-Queenslander'. And nowhere is the banana bender's pride more on display than when they're on the sporting field – except maybe when they're in the pub sipping on a XXXX and watching another Queenslander get the job done.

Supporting **the Maroons** against arch-rival the Blues.

Former Maroons rugby league player Billy Moore gave the state one of its signature sporting moments when he walked down the tunnel at Brisbane's Lang Park to take on the arch-enemy, New South Wales, in a State of Origin rugby league match in 1995. He coined the now ubiquitous battle-cry of 'Queenslander! Queenslander!' to motivate his team of underdogs. Of course, they won the series.

Banana benders remain the country's most dedicated rugby league fans, even if the 1990s success of the Reds rugby union team and the Brisbane Lions Australian Rules franchise have helped the rival codes to grow in the north. And fans of Brisbane's National Rugby League team, the Broncos, have been rewarded with five premiership wins.

In Queensland, however, it doesn't matter so much which sport you're playing, as long as you're taking on the southern states and winning. Even better if you're taking on the world.

In recent years, the state that produced the golfer Greg Norman and the tennis player and all-round Mr Nice Guy Pat Rafter has continued to turn out hot young talents. Swimming champions Grant Hackett, Giaan Rooney and Daniel Kowalski have all stared at the same black lines as they trained at Miami on the Gold Coast. The pint-sized diver Melissa Wu became the youngest-ever national title holder when she took out the 10-metre platform in 2006 – and she's

Queensland and extreme sports, like **skydiving at Toogoolawa**, go hand in hand.

WHEN IN ...

... a Queensland pub, in the summer: 'Ya garnda 'awrigin?'

... a State of Origin crowd, or the infamous Caxton Hotel near the team's home ground: 'Queenslandaaaah!'

... a holiday shack anywhere between Cape York and Tweed Heads: 'Surf's up!'

... a Surfers Paradise roadside apartment, watching the Indy Car race: 'WHAT WAS THAT?! I CAN'T HEEEAR YOU!'

... a Brisbane Lions supporters huddle: 'We are the pride of Brisbane town, / We wear maroon, blue and gold. / We will always fight for victory, / Like Fitzroy, and Bears of old,' etc (if only to demonstrate your knowledge that the team was once based in Fitzroy, Melbourne).

'Four days. Four nights. Pure power.' at the Gold Coast **Indy Car**.

only 1.35 metres tall. A 16-year-old golfer called Amy Yang, who has adopted the Gold Coast as her home, won a stunning play-off victory at the ANZ Ladies Masters in the same year.

At the annual Queensland Sport Awards, high-profile winners like the Brisbane Broncos happily share the stage with the likes of the Queensland Women's Rugby Union team and the Claxton Shield Baseball Team. After all, a winner's a winner, no matter what the shape of the ball.

As pure sporting carnivals go, however, there is none in the north quite like the annual Gold Coast Indy Car race. 'Four days. Four nights. Pure power.' goes the slogan, but for most it's four days, four nights, pure party, as the state's revheads gather to watch Australian V8 supercars and 750-horsepower championship cars from the United States race through the converted streets of Surfers Paradise at speeds of up to 380 kilometres per hour. The event generates around $60 million for the state.

Brisbane girls **The Veronicas** (inset top) perform in their home town.

A **speed knitting** competition at the Brisbane Convention Centre (inset bottom).

Inside the new **Gallery of Modern Art** (main picture).

THEFESTIVALCALENDAR

They may have a relaxed attitude to life, but no efforts are spared when Queenslanders decide to put on a show.

Woodford Folk Festival see in the New Year with 100,000 other folk music fans for six days and six nights on a rural property 70 kilometres from Brisbane.

Chinese New Year wish someone '*Kung Hei Fat Choy*' in Brisbane's cosmopolitan Fortitude Valley.

Winton Bush Poetry Competition hear the words that capture the spirit of the bush in the birthplace of 'Waltzing Matilda', Australia's unofficial national anthem.

The Dreaming Indigenous Festival a glorious celebration of traditional arts from across the country and around the world, and a five-star food and wine chef challenge.

Wintersun more than 1000 hot rods, custom-built and classic cars, and more than 100 bands and performers come to the Gold Coast in June for a retro-nostalgia fest.

Laura Dance and Cultural Festival once every two years, more than 20 communities from across the Cape York region flock to Laura's traditional dance ground, about 300 kilometres north of Cairns, to celebrate their diverse and unique talents.

The Cairns Show a dry season gathering of rides, junk food and woodchopping in the tropical north.

National Country Music Muster a talent search of bush poetry, country music and dancing, it's the Tamworth of the north, actually located near Gympie, inland from Noosa.

Ekka easier to say than the more formal 'Brisbane Exhibition', the annual Royal Queensland Show happens in August.

National Festival of Beers they say it's about 'beer education and culture', but if you believe that, you'll believe anything. It's the brainchild of the Story Bridge Hotel, Brisbane.

Brisbane Writers Festival panels and debates about genres such as science fiction, fantasy, crime writing and history.

Stomach-churning rides at the annual **Cairns Show** (above left).

The 'fire event' at the **Woodford Folk Festival** (below left).

The **Laura Festival** (right) focuses on reconciliation between the communities of Cape York and non-Aborigines.

WHAT IN THE WEIRD?

If you can't beat 'em, race 'em. That's the attitude crazy Queenslanders take to their pests. The Story Bridge Hotel, Brisbane, puts on grand **cockroach races** every Australia Day, which generally involves turning a bucket of cockroaches upside down in the middle of a circle and seeing which is first to reach the edge. A more testing event is the steeplechase race where hazards are provided by a garden hose. Previous winners have included Cocky Balboa, Guns 'n' Roaches, Crawline Hanson and Osama Bin Liner.

NATURALWONDERS

Some people have called Queensland 'God's country', and with good reason. Even those from other states would have to admit that, with its mountain ranges, reef and rainforest, it's the area of Australia most closely associated with stunning physical beauty.

The incredible Great Barrier Reef is, at 2000 kilometres, the biggest structure made by living organisms in the world, and the only living organism that can be seen with the naked eye from space. The Reef contains about 4000 different types of coral and is home to about 1500 species of fish, 4000 types of mollusc and countless types of sponges, sea worms and crustaceans. Dugong also live in its waters and humpback whales go there to breed. About 1.6 million tourists visit the Reef's marine park every year, attracted to the incredible snorkelling, diving and swimming to be had in its tropical waters.

The Queensland coast also boasts numerous idyllic islands. In the south, before the Barrier Reef, there are several large, vegetated sand islands such as North Stradbroke, Moreton and Fraser. The last of these is another World Heritage-listed site, chosen for its shifting dunes, tall rainforests and freshwater lakes, which comprise the world's largest sand island.

Closer to shore are the continental islands, so named because they would once have been part of the mainland. These include Great Keppel, most of the Whitsunday Islands, Hinchinbrook and Dunk. They have lush vegetation but also offer excellent diving and coral-gazing opportunities.

Lastly there are the coral islands like Green Island near Cairns and Heron Island off Gladstone, which are formed when parts of the reef are left above sea level. They offer spectacular diving opportunies.

CRIKEY!

Queensland's waters host many natural hazards as well as attractions. The best known is perhaps the **box jellyfish** (*Chironex fleckeri*). These invertebrates are abundant in the warm waters of northern Australia from November to April or May. Their venom is among the most deadly in the animal kingdom, and they are thought to have caused at least 63 deaths in the past hundred years or so. Once stung, people have been known to die within a very short and nasty five minutes. The excruciating pain causes many victims to go into shock and drown before reaching the shore. If you are unlucky enough to get stung, immediate medical assistance, including cardio-pulmonary resuscitation and the application of vinegar to prevent further stings, is your only hope. Even then you might suffer severe scarring.

The **irukandji** jellyfish is the box jellyfish's thumbnail-sized cousin. It is also extremely venomous. Its sting causes headaches, nausea, restlessness, sweating, vomiting, a high heart rate and blood pressure, severe pains in the arms, legs, back and kidneys, and a burning sensation of the skin and face – enough to ruin anyone's day at the beach.

The magical colours of **Whitsunday Island** (main picture).

A **hermit crab** (above right) hiding in its shell on brain coral.

Encountering the profusion of life on **Hardy Reef** in the Whitsundays (right).

Queensland's natural wonders are not confined to its coastline. Its inland also boasts pristine rainforest, mangroves, highlands and mountains. Perhaps most magnificent of all is the Wet Tropics area, a World Heritage-listed 'eco-region' which stretches between Townsville and Cooktown, covering about 32,700 square kilometres. The region offers spectacular scenery, with deep gorges, beautiful waterfalls and rainforest-fringed reefs. It is also home to a Garden of Eden-like diversity of flora and fauna – at least 390 rare and 74 threatened plants live there. About a third of all Australia's mammal species inhabit the region, including 25 rare species like the brush-tailed bettong, the spotted-tailed quoll and the yellow-bellied glider.

The rainforests also contain unique marsupials, including tree kangaroos and the evocatively named musky rat kangaroo.

The best known part of the Wet Tropics is the Daintree Rainforest, north of Cairns. It is one of the oldest rainforests on the planet and home to over 1000 species of plants, some of which are over 3000 years old. One of its most important residents is the shy cassowary, a flightless bird which fulfils the important role of seed disperser for over 100 species of rainforest plants. The bird is endangered but numbers are on the rise. It is unusual in having an extremely sharp, dagger-like claw which it can use to kill an enemy, disembowelling it with a single kick.

Queensland's other national parks come in all varieties, from the craggy green peaks of the Glass House Mountains, 70 kilometres north of Brisbane, to the roadless Simpson Desert in the heart of the country, with its vast sand dunes, some of which are 200 kilometres long.

The hot dry savanna of Boodjamulla National Park, in north-western Queensland, is the lonely home of one of the world's most important and abundant fossil deposits, the Riversleigh fossil site, which was World Heritage listed in 1994. The most ancient fossils here are 25 million years old, and they include a carnivore that is a close relative to the Tasmanian wolf (tiger).

A **green tree frog** finds itself a comfortable place to sleep.

Lush rainforest in the **Atherton Tablelands**.

SAVAGE GARDEN

In some parts of the Daintree Rainforest, it's better to look but not touch the greenery. Hanging down from the rainforest canopy, the thin spikes of the wait-a-while vine regularly tear the clothing and skin of unobservant walkers, causing a surprising amount of pain. Even worse is the stinging tree, also known as the gympie-gympie. This benign-looking plant, found in open and sunny parts of the rainforest, has hairs on its leaves and stems which, if touched, inflict a painful sting that can last up to six months. There is no antidote.

NOT-SO-LOCAL VILLAINS

The cane toad was introduced to Queensland in 1935 to control cane beetles. However, few could have predicted the havoc it would wreak. While failing to kill the beetles it was meant to eat, it happily started munching on other wildlife and poisoning larger animals that tried to eat it. The toad multiplies at a phenomenal rate and is thought to number around 200 million now. It has spread into the delicate environment of Kakadu and threatens the whole balance of Australian wildlife.

CRIKEY, IT'S A CONSERVATIONIST!

'Crikey!'

Irwin handled deadly snakes such as this **taipan** with consummate skill.

When Steve Irwin died suddenly and tragically of a stingray barb to the heart in 2006, the ex-pat feminist Germaine Greer said flippantly that the animal kingdom had finally exacted its revenge. She was in turn savaged by the Australian media.

But Greer's misapprehension was a common one. Irwin's apparently reckless handling of some of Australia's – and the world's – most deadly creatures gave some the impression that he was reckless about wildlife in general.

In his darkest moment, he was criticised for holding his baby boy Bob in one arm while feeding a 4-metre crocodile with the other. Irwin said he was in control of the situation, but from the loungerooms of Idaho, Iowa or St Kilda, that wasn't always clear.

Raised at his parents' Queensland Reptile and Fauna Park, which was later to become Australia Zoo on the Sunshine Coast, Irwin was dedicated to animals above all else.

'Danger, danger, danger!'

'We're grinnin' like flathead!'

The man who became synonymous with the word 'crikey' trapped crocodiles not for kicks, but because their population was endangered. By taking them to safer areas such as Australia Zoo and working on breeding programs, he could ensure the survival of their species. 'Every chance I get, I will put my life on the line to save crocs,' he told one interviewer. While there were once fewer than 5000 saltwater crocodiles in the wild in the Northern Territory, thanks to crocodile hunters like Steve, there are now about 70,000. Irwin even took wife Terri croc trapping on their honeymoon. Quite the romantic!

Irwin spent his TV earnings on large tracts of land in Australia, Vanuatu, Fiji and the United States to maintain them as virgin wilderness, 'like national parks', and counter the practice of land clearing in those countries.

It was a measure of both his worldwide fame and his huge contribution to wildlife that Prime Minister John Howard described Irwin as 'one of Australia's great conservation icons', and invited

Bindi Irwin continues in her father's footsteps, raising funds for wildlife charities.

'Have a look at this little beauty!'

'She's a little ripper!'

him to a barbecue for President George W. Bush in Canberra in 2003. It was widely suggested that Irwin be given a state funeral, but his father said it wouldn't be appropriate, as Steve would rather have been remembered as an 'ordinary bloke'. An ordinary bloke, however, for whom Hollywood stars sent messages of sympathy and the Prime Minister spoke at his memorial service, and, more importantly, who has inspired many millions around the world to take better care of the environment.

A seasonal creek lined with **River Red Gums**, near Hermannsburg.

NORTHERN TERRITORY

Stunning in its beauty, a place of oral traditions and

manual arts, the Top End is Australia's last wild frontier

and our closest point to Asia and the rest of the world.

It spreads a population roughly the same as that of

Hobart over a space the size of six United Kingdoms.

STATEFILE

The Northern Territory is a land of extremes: dry seasons without a cloud in the sky turn to months of rain with huge electrical storms; there are vast red dirt deserts as well as green wetlands teeming with life; and ancient Aboriginal traditions thrive next to Territorians' quirkier cultural activities.

The history of the Northern Territory is a fascinating one, full of failures, flukes, fights and fanciful ideas. Long before white men sailed to Australia, the indigenous people from the Kimberley to the Gulf of Carpentaria were trading with the Makassans from Asia,

A view of **Mitchell Street**, Darwin (above) from 1879 – now a bustling row of bars and restaurants.

A homeowner (left) returns after the devastation of **Cyclone Tracy** which hit on Christmas Day, 1974, killing 65 people.

alcohol and tobacco for the right to fish for trepang (a type of sea cucumber) and for Aboriginal labour.

White men only managed to establish a settlement on the country's unforgiving north coast after four unsuccessful attempts. Even then the new settlement only survived because it played host to the Overland Telegraph, a 3200-kilometre engineering marvel, completed in 1872, which linked Australia to Java and therefore the world.

Finding an overland route to the Top End had been the source of fierce competition. Burke and Wills failed famously in 1860–61. A year later, John McDouall Stuart returned successful, claiming the area for South Australia – it was his sixth attempt, but he never lost a man.

Gold was discovered at Pine Creek in the 1880s, but conditions were still harsh. The young colony was hit by massive cyclones in 1897 and 1937. A few years later Darwin was flattened by bombs from 188 planes of the Japanese air force – more bombs fell on Darwin than had on Pearl Harbor. The official death toll was around 243, but local rumour has it that this was far below the actual figure. The area suffered 60 further raids, the last being in 1943.

And after seeing off the Japanese, Darwin was hit by a category 4 cyclone called Tracy on Christmas Day, 1974. Tracy did $837 million in damage, killed 65 people, destroyed more than 70 per cent of Darwin's buildings and transport infrastructure and required the evacuation of more than half the city's inhabitants.

The Age called it a 'disaster of the first magnitude ... without parallel in Australia's history'. Some people never moved back. But most did. They're Territorians, after all. Any tougher, they'd rust.

The Ghan trainline, completed in 2004, carries goods and tourists between Adelaide and Darwin.

VITAL STATISTICS

NICKNAMES:	the Territory, the Top End, Outback Australia
AREA:	1,420,968 km^2 (3rd)
POPULATION:	207,700 (8th)
POPULATION DENSITY:	0.15 people per km^2 (8th)
LANDMARKS:	Uluru (Ayers Rock), Kata Tjuta (The Olgas), Kings Canyon, Devil's Marbles, Kakadu
MAIN INDUSTRIES:	mining, tourism, agriculture, art
SPORTS:	Aussie rules football, fishing, drinking
NATIONAL PARKS:	13, including Kakadu, Litchfield, Katherine Gorge, Finke Gorge, Ormiston Gorge
WORLD HERITAGE SITES:	Uluru–Kata Tjuta National Park

NORTHERN TERRITORYTODAY

The author Frank Hardy once told the story of a young man who heard the Gurindiji stockman Vincent Lingiari speak on a fundraising tour, and donated $500 to Lingiari's cause.

In 1966 Lingiari had led a walk-off of his fellow indigenous workers from Wave Hill Cattle Station, which was 'owned' by a British lord. It began as a protest against conditions and became a land claim when Lingiari pondered, in his own words, 'I bin thinking this Gurindiji land.' The donor – who said he had never before met an Aboriginal person – was a young Dr Fred Hollows.

Lingiari's ten-year quest for recognition sparked the movement that led to the 1976 passage of a federal act of parliament recognising Aboriginal land rights. Hollows would go on to spend three years visiting Aboriginal communities, providing 27,000 people with treatment for trachoma and 1000 with eye operations.

Both men's stories help to explain the predicament of modern Territorians. Many are disadvantaged, but ambitious. They want the rights of a state and the responsibilities, too. In 1998 they voted down a referendum for statehood because it didn't offer them the same number of seats in parliament as other states, even though their population is relatively tiny at just over 200,000.

They objected to the reports of a British journalist at the 2005 trial of convicted backpacker murderer Bradley John Murdoch because, they said, the stories made Territorians look like backward hicks.

They take no rubbish from nobody up north, and why should they? The Northern Territory separated from South Australia and came under Commonwealth control ten

The fireworks of **Territory Day** on 1 July celebrate the Northern Territory's acquisition of self-government.

years after federation, on 1 January 1911, and it was only granted responsible self-government in 1978.

But it is full of proud, tough people who have lived through more than people in other states could ever imagine and survived where others might have wilted. And still they can smile and offer all visitors that famous Top End hospitality.

NATURAL AMBASSADORS

The **wedge-tailed eagle** is the largest Australian raptor. It can soar to heights of 2000 metres on the warm outback thermals, proudly marking out its territory.

Another giant, the **red kangaroo**, is found only in the southern half of the Northern Territory. At up to two metres tall, it is the largest of the marsupials, able to cover huge distances over harsh terrain.

Sturt's desert rose is a cousin of the cotton plant. Able to store its own water, the pink or purple woody shrub is perfectly adapted to dry, sandy soils.

SIGNS OF GOVERNMENT

Uniquely among the states, the Northern Territory **coat of arms** features all its floral, animal and bird emblems, as well as indigenous painting (on the shield) and artefacts (the ritual tjurunga stone).

The **flag** of the Northern Territory features a Southern Cross on a black background on the left. On the right, a stylised, black-and-white

Sturt's desert rose sits on an ochre backdrop. Its seven white petals represent the six Australian states and the Northern Territory.

Darwin's **Parliament House** is on the site of the former Port Darwin Post and Telegraphic Office. With its white layers, it's known locally as the 'Wedding Cake'.

PEOPLEFILE

Hypothetically speaking, if you were to spread the 200,000 or so Territorians over their 1.4 million square kilometres, each person would have an area equal to about 1700 football fields.

Is it any wonder, then, that they have a reputation up here for being so friendly? They don't get to see other people that often!

In all seriousness, much of what makes Territorians unique comes back to the 'tyranny of distance' that stretches between many of them. Some live so far from a school that they have to receive their education at the School of the Air, which was conducted via correspondence on shortwave radio for the second half of the 20th century and has now switched mostly to wireless internet. The Alice Springs School of the Air teaches just under 100 primary schoolers spread over one million square kilometres for an hour a day, after which they endure homework with a tutor or family member.

The doctors up here come out of the air, too. As in many other states, the iconic Royal Flying Doctor Service has been providing remote communities with medical help when they need it since 1928.

About 30 per cent of Territorians are indigenous Australians, their largest communities being the Pitjantjatjara near Uluru, the Arrernte near Alice Springs, the Luritja also near Alice Springs, the Warlpiri further north and the Yolngu in eastern Arnhem Land.

With an average life expectancy at about 20 years below the non-indigenous average, and poor access to education, jobs and communications, it's the mission of community leaders like Mandawuy Yunupingu to bridge the gap. Yunupingu, who is the lead singer of the Aboriginal rock group Yothu Yindi, was the first Aborigine from Arnhem Land to earn a university degree, at Deakin University in 1988; the nation's first principal, at the Yirrkala Community School in 1990; and Australian of the Year in 1992.

Local kids cool off at the **4 Mile water hole** near Yuendumu community.

COLOURFUL CHARACTERS

You don't need to look far to find a colourful character in this part of the world, but a good place to begin might be at infamous **Daly Waters** (population 23). Its hotel is one of the oldest buildings in the Territory and has been licensed for over 100 years as a rest stop for thirsty drovers. Today, it is a bona fide tourist attraction, filled with the accumulated paraphernalia of thousands of travellers, from flags to cash, ID cards and various items of intimate apparel – the rules are: if you lose at pool, you lose your underwear and it joins the display.

Or further along the Stuart Highway is the small town of Wycliffe Well – Australia's UFO sighting capital. In 2002 the *Sun-Herald* reported it was the number five spot in the world for encounters of the unidentified flying kind.

Coral Beebe on the **family property** Ucharonidge, which is 250 km north of Tennant Creek.

CITY STYLE

I n Peter Goldsworthy's *Maestro*, a book many a high school student has been forced to study, Darwin is described as: 'That small, tropical hothouse of a port, half outback, half oriental, lying at the tip of northern Australia.'

If the heat doesn't get you, the beer will, they say. It's a rare human being who visits Darwin and leaves without having gone at least a bit 'troppo'. For a long time it was a place where people went to run from something or someone, giving the city an outlaw feel despite its beautiful setting. Like the saltwater crocs that lurk at the edge of its white sandy beaches, it was a paradise with a hint of danger.

Today Darwin is a family-friendly, economically prosperous town riding on the back of mining and tourism incomes. It also supports a huge number of government workers and military personnel, all of whom require the usual civilised services you'd find in any city. Many residents are Greeks, Filipinos, Timorese and Chinese; even more are Aborigines or Torres Strait Islanders. And, geographically, it's closer to the capitals of East Timor, Papua New Guinea and Indonesia than it is to Canberra, so its racial mix reflects its place on the map. According to recent reports, the city is now attracting more people than ever; young professionals are heading north in droves – the average age of the population is around 32.

But Darwin still retains a sense of Darwin time. It enjoys more daylight hours than any other state capital – 8.4 on average – and when the weather is good, people get out and make the most of it. When the day's work is over, the city does what it does best. Whether at Mindil Beach market, the Trailer Boat Club or the Ski Club, it's time to get out your stubby holder, sink a few beers and watch the sun drop into the Arafura Sea.

DID YOU KNOW?
Territorians will proudly tell you that they have one of the highest recorded **alcohol consumption** rates in the world. In 2001 the National Drug Research Institute estimated it at 1120 standard drinks per person, per year. Darwinians have even been known to joke that the two huge pipes running along the Stuart Highway into Darwin pump beer straight from the Carlton Brewery in Melbourne.

There is a huge variety of **delicious food** at Darwin's popular Mindil Beach market, but for something genuinely vernacular, what could be more local than the Roadkill Cafe. With a motto of 'You kill it, we grill it', the Roadkill makes a meal out of traffic mishaps such as croc, roo, emu, buffalo, camel and possum. What could be more patriotic in a country that eats both of the animals on its coat of arms?

Darwin Central Hotel (above left) and the corner of Knuckey and Smith streets in the city centre.

Locals enjoy the **sunset at the Ski Club** (main picture) – 'ski' as in water, not snow.

Cattle (above) at a Northern Territory station. Many are transported live from the port of Darwin to Indonesia, where they can be killed according to Muslim tradition.

Mangoes (left) thrive in the tropical heat of the Top End. The season starts around late September.

COUNTRYSTYLE

For around a century, the Territory's primary source of income was cattle grazing, and stations here are still going strong, adapting all the time. However, mining has taken over as the big earner, supplemented by newer undertakings such as tourism, mango growing and camel farming.

When pastoralists and settlers pushed north into the Territory in the 1900s, they took over some of the planet's largest tracts of land for grazing and employed Aboriginal men as stockmen and drovers. They were skilled cowboys, but often not very well paid. Now, 40 years after Vincent Lingiari and his Gurindiji mob walked off Wave Hill Station, some of the Territory's cattle stations are wholly Aboriginal-run or -owned.

stray bulls in the right direction or pin them down so they can be secured. However, horse sense is still necessary for the finer work; horses cause less stress to the cattle.

Ross Morton at Henbury Station stocks **camels**; many are exported, others are used domestically for their meat.

On 21st century stations, changes have occurred in other ways. Farmers here have particularly prospered from Brahman cattle as opposed to traditional European breeds, because of their ability to withstand the heat and their tolerance of lack of water. The seasonal muster is often helped by motorbikes, helicopters or a 'bullcatcher' – a battered 4WD with reinforced bumpers to nudge

Whereas the cattle stations make use of the territory's wide open spaces, the area around Katherine and Darwin offers a more fertile climate for farmers. Here, the mango industry is booming. Over the last ten years it has grown 640 per cent and the territory's 550 growers now bring in around $35 million to the economy, even though over half their trees have yet to reach full maturity.

SPORTFILE

Perhaps it's the climate, or perhaps it's the ready supply of alcohol, but sport in the Top End is a bloody good excuse for a party.

Pumaralli (above) celebrate their win at the March 2006 Tiwi Islands Grand Final.

The **Darwin to Ambon Yacht Race** (right) covers 600 nautical miles to Indonesia.

Jamie and David Gulpilil attending the premier of *Ten Canoes*.

coming from top side'. Sales figures for indigenous art and artefacts at one Melbourne auction house grew from $100,000 to more than $7 million in the past decade alone. They are worth much more in cultural terms.

But perhaps nothing gives a better impression of the vibrancy of Aboriginal culture than the amazing festivals and gatherings of the territory. Every year the yidaki (didgeridoo) calls together over 20 clan groups of north-east Arnhem Land to Garma. Staged by the Yolngu people, this festival happens when people bring different ideas and values together. Dance and song, visual art, yidaki classes, bush tucker and medicine, spear-making and -throwing — all this knowledge is shared. At Walking with Spirits, in southern Arnhem Land, there are similar celebrations, where old and young perform on the shores of a billabong near the Wugularr community. Behind the stage, the cliffs might be lit with different colours while candles are floated on the water. Some performers might have to be coaxed out of their shyness, while children run and tumble in the sand around them, giving the whole event a joyful informality.

involved to re-learn, preserve and pass on their culture. For audiences, it was an insight into the culture of Arnhem Land.

De Heer collected the award for best picture with his co-director Peter Djiggir, but gave credit to the actor David Gulpilil (also in *Storm Boy*, 1976, and *Crocodile Dundee*, 1986), who paved the way for black actors and whose son Jamie acted in *Ten Canoes*: 'Thank you for pestering me for years to make a film with your land and your people,' de Heer announced to the auditorium and nationwide TV audience.

The movie also won a special jury prize at the 2006 Cannes Film Festival. Never before have Australia's indigenous film-makers been so celebrated.

In the visual arts, however, the culturati have been celebrating the Top End's artists for a little longer. The works of Albert Namatjira and the late Emily Kame Kngwarreye have been highly sought after for years, and in 2001 the National Gallery of Australia paid a record $778,750 for Rover Thomas's painting 'All that big rain

Wilfred Wurrawilya and Thomas Amagula perform a **traditional dance**, Groote Eylandt.

NATURALWONDERS

Clouds and green scrubland surround **Uluru**.

Travelling thousands of kilometres across a featureless landscape, you might think there is little to impress in the Northern Territory, until you suddenly come across wonders on a mammoth scale. Photographs of the territory rarely do its landscape justice. Its sights have to been seen to be believed.

Rising out of the flat red desert near the geographical centre of Australia, Uluru looks like the country's giant red heart. Many stories surround it; some may be true, some definitely aren't.

That Uluru is the world's largest monolith is a myth. Mount Augustus in Western Australia is more than twice as big. Also Uluru is not strictly a single rock but only the tip of a vast underground formation. However, with a circumference of nine kilometres and a height of 348 metres, Uluru is still pretty impressive.

And it is jaw-droppingly beautiful, morphing from pink to mauve to red, blue and brown as the light changes through the day. When the rains come, they fall like a quicksilver curtain over the rock, before running down its wrinkles into waterholes and desert.

Only 50 kilometres away, Kata Tjuta, meaning 'many heads' in Pitjantjatjara, is not as large but is higher, at 546 metres, and equally mysterious. Long known to Westerners as the Olgas – after Olga, the Queen of Württemberg – the area regained its Aboriginal name in 1993, as did Uluru, which had been named after Sir Henry Ayers, a Chief Secretary of South Australia.

The explorer Ernest Giles, who renamed them in 1872, described Kata Tjuta as 'minarets, giant cupolas and monstrous domes ... huge memorials to the ancient times of the earth'. His description of Uluru was slightly less adequate – 'the remarkable pebble'.

Aborigines say Uluru and Kata Tjuta were formed during the Tjukurpa (creation period), but legends vary as to how it actually happened. One says that when a tribe of ancestral spirits failed to turn up to the feast of another tribe, a battle ensued, ending in the death of both tribes' leaders. The earth rose up in grief at the bloodshed, giving us Uluru.

There are Luritja and Pitjantjatjara paintings and carvings thousands of years old at the base of Uluru, confirming the sacredness of the place since time immemorial. And some tourists have discovered Uluru's power for themselves. Tempted to take rocks from the area as souvenirs, many have returned them with letters detailing the misfortunes they have suffered because of it.

Another of the Territory's – and the country's – most impressive parks is Kakadu, king of parks. The size of Switzerland, it has won World Heritage listing and contains all the major habitats of the Top End, from wetlands to woodlands and rugged rock, as well as 5000 Aboriginal art sites. But Kakadu is rich in other ways. In an area that Aboriginal people have long called 'the sickness country', uranium was discovered in 1953. Conservationists and capitalists continue to debate how much of it should be mined.

FIVE OF THE BEST ... NATIONAL PARKS

Ormiston Gorge a place where fish bury themselves in the mud and wait for rain to fall again.

Finke Gorge its beautiful Palm Valley is a refuge for ancient cycads and the 5000-year-old palm *Livistona mariae* – the colony is separated from its nearest neighbours by about 1000 kilometres.

Litchfield 100 kilometres south of Darwin, little-known Litchfield's waterfalls plummet all year round, providing welcome swimming holes in the dry.

Nitmiluk National Park ride a flat-bottomed boat or canoe through the Katherine Gorge and fish for barramundi in the primordial silver waters.

Devil's Marbles outside Tennant Creek, this conservation reserve is a random pile of almost-perfect spheres that geologists say are granite boulders, but which Aboriginal legend says are eggs laid by the mythical Rainbow Serpent.

The red dirt road from **Owen Springs to Boggy Hole**.

The lush wetlands of **Bathurst Island**, in the Tiwi Island group.

WILDTERRITORY

The Northern Territory is home to about 400 species of birds, 150 species of mammals, 300 species of reptiles, 50 species of frogs, 60 species of freshwater fish and several hundred species of marine fish. Not bad, huh?

About 280, or one-third, of all of Australia's bird species, including the endangered Gouldian finch and red goshawk, one of the world's rarest birds of prey, live in the area of Kakadu and Arnhem Land. This, of course, makes it a common habitat for a slightly peculiar subspecies of human, the twitcher. Bird Week is held here every August.

The peculiar looking **thorny devil** isn't as aggressive as it looks – if frightened it will hide its head between its legs.

LOCAL LEGENDS

They may be cold-blooded killers, but even salties evoke a fondness in Territorians. In the late 1970s, **Sweetheart**, a 5.2-metre, 780-kilogram male, was suspected of attacking passing boats in the Finniss River – the engine noise seemed to annoy him. So the Parks and Wildlife people decided to move him on. Sadly, a dose of sedative and a snagged rope caused him to drown during the capture. One of his particularly brave captors actually jumped in the water to attempt something akin to mouth-to-mouth, but to no avail. So Sweetheart was stuffed and put on display in the Northern Territory Museum and Art Gallery, Darwin, where he is one of its most popular attractions.

Even nature's timetable is unique here. Local Aborigines describe six seasons, which indicate when to look for certain foods. In the *gurrung* (hot, dry August to mid-October), the pandanus ripen and sea turtles lay eggs. Bushfires are lit to reduce the risk of larger burns and improve hunting. In *gudjewg* (the 'true' wet of January and February), it's time to collect goose eggs. And in *wurrgeng* (the 'cold' of June to July), sweet-nectared grevillea, 'the bush lolly', keeps the kids quiet.

The **intermediate egret** is a common sight in the wetlands.

CRIKEY!

Freshwater crocodiles, or 'freshies', may look scary, but they're nothing in comparison to 'salties'. The name **saltwater crocodile** is unhelpfully misleading as, in fact, salties can be found in fresh water as well. Although large – males grow to around four or five metres, sometimes more – their reactions are many times faster than ours, and they are adept at bursting onto a river bank to catch their prey. They can even jump straight up out of the water for up to two-thirds of their body length. Despite their fearsome potential, they only kill an average of one person a year in Australia, compared to bees which kill around ten.

Established as a colony only because the British feared the French might get there first, Western Australia is now booming. It is rich in myriad ways – from the spectacular Kimberley, Ningaloo Reef and Shark Bay to its almost limitless space, mineral wealth and an easygoing cosmopolitan lifestyle, it's easy to see why residents think West is best.

The Pinnacles rock formations at Nambung National Park.

WESTERN AUSTRALIA

STATEFILE

The first Western Australians arrived in the area 40,000 to 60,000 years ago. Sea levels were much lower then and they may even have walked part of the way from Asia.

Of course, the first Europeans arrived much later, but still long before they made it to the east coast. In 1616 the Dutch explorer Dirk Hartog landed at what is now known as Cape Inscription, Dirk Hartog Island. In 1644 another Dutchman, Abel Tasman, charted the coast as far as the Gulf of Carpentaria, and in 1699 the English explorer and pirate William Dampier sailed down the western coast and came into Shark Bay. Dampier reported the land as being stark and barren, so no attempts at settlement were made for many years.

By 1826, however, the British began to fear that the French would establish a colony on the west of

Louis Julien Jacottet's view of **King George Sound** (above), painted in 1833.

A map of **New Holland** (left), drawn in 1680 by Johannes van Keulen.

DID YOU KNOW?

The region's position, close to the Indian Ocean trading routes, meant that several Europeans landed here before reaching the east coast, often when boats arrived accidentally, en route to Batavia (Jakarta).

In 1629 the *Batavia* struck a reef of the Abrolhos. Skipper Francisco Pelsaert took the ship's small boat to Batavia for rescue but when he returned three months later many of the survivors had been murdered in a bloody mutiny.

the continent. They took action by sending Major Edmund Lockyer to claim the land around King George Sound, which became the settlement of Albany. Three years later Captain James Stirling established a colony on the Swan River, which was to grow into Fremantle and the capital Perth. Stirling became Lieutenant Governor of Australia's first free colony, something its inhabitants are proud of to this day. Convicts did, however, provide a free labour force.

VITAL STATISTICS

NICKNAME:	the Wildflower State
AREA:	2,529,875 km² (1st)
POPULATION:	2,050,900 (4th)
POPULATION DENSITY:	0.79 people per km² (7th)
LANDMARKS:	Kalgoorlie gold mines, the Kimberley, Monkey Mia, the Swan River, the Swan Bell Tower, Valley of the Giants, Wave Rock
INDUSTRIES:	mining (iron, alumina, natural gas, nickel and gold) and agriculture (wheat, barley and sheep)
SPORTS:	AFL, soccer, netball, basketball
NATIONAL PARKS:	96, including Nambung (the Pinnacles), Walpole-Nornalup, Karijini, Serpentine, Porongurup
WORLD HERITAGE SITES:	Purnululu National Park, Shark Bay

The colony was sparsely populated until gold was discovered – first at Halls Creek in 1885, then at Coolgardie in 1892 and Kalgoorlie in 1893. The population surged as people from everywhere arrived to try their luck.

The gold rush and the wealth it created lent weight to the state's pleas for self-government, which all other states had by then. It was granted by Queen Victoria in 1890. As seams of gold were mined out, the wealth started to peter out. The reliable industries of wool and wheat picked up some of the slack, but when the prices of these two commodities fell during the Depression, the state's economy collapsed.

During the two World Wars, Western Australia was of great strategic importance and many of its towns, notably Broome, which in 1942 was bombed by Japanese planes, are steeped in wartime history in the form of abandoned bunkers and dusty military airstrips.

Following the war, the state enjoyed enormous financial growth from the cattle trade, the emergence of the pearling industry near Broome, and agriculture and whaling. In the 1970s discoveries of oil and gas, as well as some of the world's largest iron ore deposits, rocketed the state into an economic boom which continues today.

WESTERN AUSTRALIATODAY

Western Australia is big, in every sense of the word. It has a huge landmass, so big you could fit Texas and New Zealand into its borders. It is the largest sub-national entity (part of a country) after the Sakha Republic in Russia.

The state's economy is also big, dependent as it is on the huge mining industry, especially iron, alumina, nickel, gold and natural gas. Western Australia is the world's third-largest iron ore producer and it is also a leading alumina extractor, producing about 20 per cent of all the alumina on earth. Diamonds are also extracted from around Argyle in the north-west, and coal for domestic power production is mined at Collie. In recent years, tourism has grown, and the state also has a strong agricultural sector, especially in wheat, barley and sheep products.

These treasures, combined with a worldwide resources boom, have made WA rich – it has the highest per capita output of the states. Western Australia now punches well above its weight on a national scale, providing 40 per cent of foreign export revenues for the whole country. The riches have brought low unemployment, high income, and strong corporate activity. The economic boom is so pronounced that there is a labour shortage and the state government has launched a campaign urging other Australians to 'go west'.

Despite all these resources, much of the state is pretty barren, with only one really fertile patch in the south-west. The geography of the central inland is revealed in names such as the Little Sandy and Great Sandy Deserts. The rugged north does receive good rainfall, but the country here is wild, producing the stunning gorges and waterfalls of the Kimberley.

The natural beauty, economic boom and easygoing pace of life, combined with a young population, make for an incredibly idyllic lifestyle. That's probably the reason most Westralians don't mind their state being so isolated – it's all the better for them to enjoy.

SIGNS OF GOVERNMENT

On the **coat of arms**, two kangaroos hold a shield showing a black swan. Above them is the British Crown, and the boomerangs they hold represent the Aboriginal nations of WA.

The **flag** combines the Union Jack with the black swan badge on a blue background.

The granite and freestone building of **Parliament House** on Harvest Terrace was opened in 1904.

NATURAL AMBASSADORS

In 1697 the Dutch explorer, Vlamingh, noted the large number of **black swans** on the waters that would become known as the Swan River, and since the Swan River Colony was established in 1829 the birds have come to represent the state.

The striking red and green **kangaroo paw** is found naturally only in Western Australia.

Once widespread across southern Australia, the **numbat** is now only found in south-west Western Australia. It is a small, stripy creature that lives on termites and the occasional ant.

PEOPLEFILE

S andgropers are pretty ugly creatures, with long bodies and short legs, and spend their lives burrowing through the sand. They are also Western Australians, a separate sub-species of Aussie – and proud of it.

Life here is a bit different from the rest of the country. For starters, the sun rises over the desert and sets in the ocean, which seems all back-to-front for the majority of us. What's more, it's a different ocean: the warm, windy Indian as opposed to the vast, brisk Pacific.

Where the Swan River meets that ocean, entrepreneurs founded Australia's first free colony in 1829. In 1901 they were the last to give in to Federation. Then, feeling they were being ignored by the east, they voted to go it alone. The appeal to Her Majesty in 1933 didn't succeed, and Western Australians today still exhibit secessionist tendencies. Ironically, they have more reason than ever to break away, as their resources-based economy drives Australia's foreign exchange but gets inferior representation in Canberra.

Western Australians are miners, magnates, cowboys, golddiggers, pearl divers, wheat farmers, sailors, fishermen and corporate raiders. They are big movers in the geographical sense, too. WA has a higher percentage of foreign-born citizens than any other capital city.

They also have the highest overseas migration rates in the nation. But why anyone would want to leave is a mystery – after all, the men's magazine *FHM* says the Cottesloe Beach Hotel is home to the best-looking women in Australia, and Perth has more millionaires per capita than anywhere in the world. Meanwhile, some indigenous Western Australians in the Pilbara and the Kimberley have only made contact with the marauding whites in the past century.

Such are the contrasts of Australia's wild west.

COLOURFUL CHARACTERS

Prince Leonard and Princess Shirley
only in Western Australia would you find secessionists from the secessionists. Prince Leonard and Princess Shirley of Hutt River Principality founded Australia's most determined micro-nation on 18,500

acres north of Perth in 1970 because they were unhappy with wheat pricing. They now claim an impressive worldwide citizenry of 13,000; don't pay tax; accept tourists and stamp their passports; approve their own developments; and export coins, stamps and agricultural products. The federal government has so far let them be.

MOST LIKELY TO SAY:

Here comes the Doctor.

We're fine here on our own, thanks.

Who's up for a Sunday sesh?

LEAST LIKELY TO SAY:

I feel sorry for that Rose Hancock-Porteous ...

Actually, I'm not interested in real estate.

I'd love to see a sunrise over the ocean.

Aboriginal **traditional owner of Nyikina country**, John Watson, shows his son and grandchildren his special lands in the Kimberley.

CITYSTYLE

Perth's founder Captain James Stirling said in 1829 that the city was 'as beautiful as anything of this kind I have ever witnessed', and it's only become lovelier since then. Most of us know that Perth is the most isolated city in the world, closer to Jakarta than any fellow state capital, but its isolation hasn't stopped it from becoming a modern, dynamic city. Now the fastest growing city in Australia, it is home to about 1.5 million people, around three-quarters of the state's residents.

The city is blessed with beauty; elegant parks, the graceful Swan River and fine colonial architecture combine to give it a quiet, peaceful charm. One of Perth's newest and most visually arresting attractions is the Bell Tower, on the edge of the Swan River. Actually one of the largest musical instruments on earth, the tower houses the twelve bells of London's St Martin in the Fields Church, gifted to Western Australia to mark the country's bicentenary.

The city's colonial buildings are equally fascinating. Government House, located on St Georges Terrace, was the last of several unsuccessful attempts to build a house for the colony's governor. The first was reportedly so badly constructed that when it rained the governor had to use an umbrella while replying to official correspondence. With the final effort, however, the builders got it right, as visitors to the remarkable Tudor-style, two-coloured brick building will agree.

rn developments include the Burswood Casino and Entertainment complex, where international acts and sport events are held, and the East Perth Re-Development Area. Also called Riverside, this area is home to the WACA (Western Australian Cricket Association), Gloucester Park and Queens Gardens, and

destined to be an entertainment, commercial and residential district. It will eventually include an indoor stadium and pedestrian malls.

South of the city is the port-town of Fremantle, with its bustling café strip and cosmopolitan atmosphere, largely due to the large number of Greek, Italian, Macedonian and Croatian immigrants who have settled here. It has many buildings still standing from its convict past, most notably the Fremantle Prison, which is said to be haunted, and the WA Maritime Museum, where the remains of the *Batavia*, which was wrecked off the coast in 1629, can be seen.

The **Perth skyline** (main picture).

The **Swan Bell Tower** (left), overlooking the Swan River, was completed in 2001.

The port reflected in the windows of the **Maritime Centre** (above right).

UNREAL**ESTATES**

There are more millionaires in Perth than in any other capital city on earth, and millionaires need mansions. The city's corporate cowboys, fuelled by the resources boom, have driven Perth real estate prices up by 39 per cent in the past three years. Perth has replaced Sydney as the most expensive city in which to buy property in Australia.

Stories of people sleeping in the street to secure off-the-plan apartments are now common. The hottest suburbs are North Fremantle, East Perth and City Beach, but the old money is in suburbs such as Peppermint Grove, Dalkeith and Mosman Park. Peppermint Grove, named for the peppermint trees that line its streets, is home to the prominent business families of Bunning, Burt, Forrest and, more recently, Mitsui.

Of course, all that money does not necessarily buy taste.

Probably the best example of outlandish architecture in Western Australia is Prix d'Amour, which was built by the late Lang Hancock, a mining magnate, for his Filipino-born wife, Rose Porteous. It is a lavish 16-block mansion overlooking the Swan River, modelled after the Tara plantation from *Gone with the Wind*. It was reportedly the setting for many large parties at which the two lovers would 'dance into the night'.

Angela Bennett, the daughter of Hancock's former business partner, Peter Wright, also owns some seriously luxurious Perth architecture. Her 10,000 square metre mansion in Mosman Park was valued at $55 million by *BRW*. The property features a guest house, separate caretaker's quarters, both with views over the Swan River, and a private jetty with three-level boatshed.

The housing boom isn't confined to Perth. Another emerging trend is the migration of buyers south of the city to coastal towns such as Mandurah, now dubbed the state's version of Noosa. Mandurah and Geraldton, to the north, are also popular with miners who fly out of the outback to spend their time off by the coast.

Dunsborough, about 2.5 hours south-west of Perth, is another beachside resort where prices have escalated rapidly in the past ten years, with beachfront land values going up more than 400 per cent in that time.

A multi-millionaire's mansion (above) among the orange groves and vineyards of **Chittering Valley**.

On Jutland Parade, Dalkeith, this **luxury pad** (main picture) was designed by Yael Kurlansky.

EAT, DRINK, DANCE

Western Australia is blessed with an abundance of high quality produce, and no one knows this better than the restaurateurs of Perth, who exploit the good food and excellent weather to create world-class dining experiences.

Jackson's in Highgate is often described as Perth's finest restaurant. Run by English chef Neal Jackson, it is famous for its 'dego' menu, which, Jackson explains, is Australian for 'degustation'. Halo restaurant, on the Swan River, is another upmarket choice. It specialises in contemporary Australian, particularly seafood and game, and the chefs pride themselves on making absolutely every-thing on the premises.

Perth's seafood is world-class, unsurprising when you consider the large crayfishing industry its waters support. As a consequence, its seafood restaurants are world-famous. The Loose Box is a French restaurant in semi-rural Mundaring, east of the city. Its classic menu includes local ingredients such as yabbies and their close cousin, the marron. Fuche, a sister restaurant to one in London's Piccadilly Circus, is a hip, retro-style venue with its own DJ. For more old-school, traditional dining, gourmands head to the National Trust-listed Melbourne Hotel in Perth, famous for its degustation menu.

The **Loose Box** restaurant, Mundaring.

In Northbridge, Perth's diverse cultural mix can be seen in the choice of foods on offer – from excellent Italian espresso at European Foods to Greek delicacies at Kakulas Brothers. Cocktails and tapas at the Box Deli are also legendary.

Northbridge is also the nightlife location of choice for Perth's hot young things, with bars and nightclubs such as Kremlin, O2 and the Post Office all attracting a hip, buzzing crowd. For popular bands and live music, the Brass Monkey and Brasserie and the Metropolis City Nightclub go off most nights, as does the Aberdeen Hotel.

The West End of the CBD has also grown in recent years, and is now a very fashionable post-office spot for city workers, with plenty of boutique breweries to choose from. Further towards West Perth are even more stylish venues such as Onyx and Black Tom's, where punters can enjoy that most elegant of combinations: champagne and fresh oysters.

But by far the favourite form of socialising for locals is still the Sunday session. Some of the best venues for 'seshing' include the Leederville Hotel, the Ocean Beach Hotel (or simply the OBH) in North Cottesloe and the Cottesloe Beach Hotel.

Having a coldie at the **Sail & Anchor Hotel**.

FIVE OF THE BEST ... BOUTIQUE BREWERIES

Little Creatures on Fremantle's Fishing Boats Harbour, this brewery takes its name from the 'little creatures' (aka yeast) that go into its award-winning brews. Everyone loves the pale ale.

Duckstein Brewery on West Swan Road this German beer garden and restaurant offers a little piece of Bavaria, sandgroper-style.

Feral Brewery on Haddrill Road in Baskerville, the Feral is well known for its food, wine and beer. Patrons can watch the micro-brewery in action.

Ironbark Brewery in Caversham, this brewery produces a variety of flavoursome thirst-quenchers such as wheat brew, Munich ale, Indian pale ale and Vienna lager and stout.

Elmar's in the Valley all beers here are made in accordance with the German Purity Law of 1516, which stipulates beer must be made from water, hops, malt and yeast and nothing else.

Perth locals spend a great deal of time outdoors: cycling, swimming, walking and stopping to smell the roses – or at least the wildflowers.

TIMEOUTDOORS

With its Mediterranean climate and relatively low rainfall, it's no surprise Perth locals spend a great deal of time outdoors: cycling, swimming, walking and stopping to smell the roses – or at least the wildflowers of the city's parks and gardens.

There's no shortage of nature on display in Perth. On the Esplanade, between the city and the river, is the Allan Green Plant Conservatory, which houses a glorious mix of tropical and semi-tropical plants. Visitors who want to see the city's famous black swans head to Lake Monger, north-west of the city centre.

Kings Park is the biggest and most famous of Perth's gardens. Reserved as parkland in 1831 by the colony's first surveyor general, it also boasts sweeping lawns, a botanic garden and many of the wildflowers for which WA is famous.

Nature has also carved its own outdoor playgrounds. On the banks of the meandering Swan River there are more than 50 kilometres of riverside pathways for roller-blading, jogging and cycling. At beaches such as Lancelin, north of the city, wind-surfing and sand-boarding are popular. Just south of Perth at places such as Rockingham and Mandurah, there is excellent whale-watching, foreshore picnicking and crabbing.

One of the great weekend traditions, however, has a much more competitive focus: going to see the West Coast Eagles or the Fremantle Dockers play at Subiaco Oval.

English eccentric, Lloyd Scott (right), riding his **penny farthing** bike in Kings Park to raise money for cancer research, in 2004.

Kings Park, the lake and its **Pioneer Memorial** (left).

BEACHLIVING

With a 12,000-kilometre coast, which is more than a third of the country's total, WA has a lot of beach. Whether being sociable by the sea or sunbaking by themselves, sandgropers have the best of beach living.

Considering Perth's higher-than-average number of sunshine hours, it's no surprise that you'll find quite a few of them groping the sand on one of the area's 19 beaches. These, of course, offer plenty of opportunities to be sociable – whatever you're into.

Some, like Trigg Beach and Scarborough Beach, are great for a surf, whether it's of the body, board, kite or wind variety. Scarborough also stages regular volleyball competitions, and, if you're not too tired at the end of the day, this is the place to find serious seaside nightlife.

Those looking for a more relaxing time might head to Mettams Pool. With no swell during summer and a friendly atmosphere, it's a

THE ROTTNEST LOTTERY

Gorgeous Rottnest Island, a ferry ride away from Perth, is ringed by pristine white sands and crystal-clear turquoise waters. Cars are few and far between, so most people get around by bicycle. And if that wasn't idyllic enough, cute, furry little quokkas pop up among the eucalypts. It's so beautiful and popular that the only way to secure one of its delightful wooden cabins or sandstone cottages for Christmas or Easter is by lottery – a year in advance. The results are announced in the *West Australian*.

Boating off **Rottnest Island**, with Perth in the distance.

Indiana on Cottesloe Beach is a Perth icon, which has had a recent facelift.

favourite with families. Little kids and big kids have fun snorkelling on its surrounding reef.

Cottesloe Beach, with its crystal clear waters and pine tree-lined beach promenade, is one of the most famous in the state, if not the country. As well as offering great swimming, it has a vibrant café and restaurant culture. Many a civilised afternoon has been spent partaking of refreshment at the Indiana tea house, a bathhouse-turned-restaurant with colonial Asian décor, complete with cane chairs and wooden floors.

But if you want to throw caution to the wind, and your clothes along with it, head to Swanbourne's nudist beach. Not only can you expose all your bits, you can expose yourself to gun fire – there's a live rifle range behind the beach.

FIVE OF THE BEST … DOG BEACHES

Leighton Beach more properly called Mosman Beach, this is a great place to exercise. The gently shelving shallows are perfect for doggy paddling.

North Beach swirling surf and fallen rocks make for a bracing walk, with plenty of nooks and crannies to explore.

Scarborough with so much space for running, what self-respecting dog could not like this beach?

South Beach what this Fremantle gem lacks in space, it makes up for in variety. There's grass as well as sand – both great for a game of fetch. And a scattering of seaweed provides some interesting smells.

South-City an expansive stretch with beautiful scenery to keep the owners amused. It's near Swanbourne, however, so watch out for men playing with their weapons (see left).

DREAMDESTINATIONS

For those who like to get away from the crowds, Western Australia has big skies, wide open spaces and long reefs, and some of the most exotic and exciting beaches in the world.

Broome, on the Kimberley coast, is the well-known getaway, with its palm-fringed shores and cosmopolitan history. Aborigines were the first to trade in the region's pearl shells, but later Europeans, South Sea Islanders, Japanese and Chinese all flocked to the region. The notion of pearl luggers working the Indian Ocean may be romantic, but for many years the reality was much harsher – poorly paid divers risked death on a daily basis. Now, however, the pearls are mostly cultured and farmed. The town is still seen as the Pearl Capital of the World; it produces up to $150 million worth a year.

Tourism is Broome's other chief industry. The sunsets and camel trains of Cable Beach are a key attraction, but there are also a host of luxury spas and sanctuaries, set in tropical oases and offering as much relaxation as you can take. Cable Beach Resort, for example, is the epitome of swanky style, with its oriental architecture and manicured lawns.

At the other end of the state, in the south-west corner, is yet more pristine coastline. Margaret River is a mecca for surfers the world over. Surfing legend Nat Young once described the break there as

Playing cricket on **Cable Beach**, Broome.

'epic', and world surfing champ Kelly Slater called it 'one of the world's finest'. The Salomon Masters competition is held here annually. The town itself offers relaxed, slightly alternative living, surrounded by some of the country's best vineyards.

Spectacular coastline characterises the rugged south coast. With a rich whaling history and its current status as the region's commercial centre, Albany is bustling. Today, whales swim peacefully off its grey granite coves, joined by human divers attracted to the wreck of the HMAS *Perth*. Esperance is another popular resort. Norfolk pines line the town's foreshore, framing a scene of dazzling blue waters and squeaky white sand.

SEASCAPES: BUSSELTON JETTY

First opened in 1865, Busselton jetty (main picture) was built to load ships with the area's precious timber. Shifting sands over the years required it to be extended, until it reached 2 kilometres and became the longest jetty in the Southern Hemisphere. Horses pulled the log wagons along the jetty, until a rail line was added in the early 20th century. Now the jetty hosts more leisurely pursuits: walking, fishing and watching the artificial reef from its underwater observatory. It's also an excellent spot to dive-bomb your friends.

COUNTRYSTYLE

This is a state with a whole lot of land. Much of it, however, isn't so great for growing things. Besides the wheatfields of the Midlands, the state's crops tend to huddle in the fertile southern corner. Less fussy sheep and cattle, of course, have more freedom to roam, and the central and northern lands, which look barren on the surface, conceal vast deposits of mineral wealth.

The Swan Valley is the state's oldest wine-growing region, and many of its vineyards are still owned by descendants of the European migrants who settled in the area from the 1920s. Today it is home to internationally famous wineries like Sandalford and Houghton, known for its white burgundy. The Swan Valley is also renowned for its 'stickies' – sweet wines made from grape varieties such as dolcetto and pedro.

The classic Mediterranean climate of the Margaret River region, with its cool, frost-free winters, moisture-retaining soil, low summer rainfall and slow ripening period, is ideal for grape-growing. The wine industry in the area is a new one, with the first vines planted only in 1967, but already the region has 110 wineries, and is known for its cabernets.

One of the best wineries here is the multi-award-winning Voyager Estate. Set in a white-gabled, Cape Dutch-style building, amid incredible rose gardens, the chefs of its restaurant carefully match the estate's wines with local produce. The winery also hosts theatre, such as French farce, over dinner.

The region offers more than just wine to expand western waist-lines. Margaret River Venison supplies deer meat throughout Australia, and the Margaret River Dairy Company provides brie, camembert, blue and cheddar cheese to go with all that wine. That other great dairy product, chocolate, is also produced here, and recently, the Wine & Truffle Company in Manjimup has been doing its best to steal business from the more established farms of France. Further north, in the state's wheat belt, the town of New Norcia is home to a Spanish Benedictine monastery, which produces olive oil and sourdough bread using traditional methods.

Dom Christopher, a Benedictine monk from New Norcia, inspects a glass of **Benedictine Abbey wine** from the Bindoon Vineyard, north of Perth.

Capel Vale
Cape Mentelle
Cullen
Devil's Lair
Houghton
Lamont's
Leeuwin Estate
Moss Brothers
Plantagenet
Riverbank Estate
Stella Bella
Suckfizzle
Vasse Felix
Voyager Estate
Wignalls Wines

LOCAL LEGENDS

A few months after Kalgoorlie's Palace Hotel opened in 1897, a 22-year-old US mining engineer went in for a drink and fell in love with one of the barmaids. The engineer was **Herbert Hoover**, who later became the US president. Accounts of the romance vary and her identity slipped into obscurity, but when Hoover left after a year, she stayed in his memory. He sent her an elaborate gift – a huge carved mirror, which she donated to the pub. It is there still, underneath the grand staircase. Beside it is a framed copy of a poem the future president wrote for his beloved: 'And I spent my soul in kisses, crushed upon your scarlet mouth/Oh! My red-lipped, sun-browned sweetheart, dark-eyed daughter of the south ...' Alas, Hoover's love did not last. He later married his American sweetheart.

THE WILD WEST

The Western Australian outback, stretching from the goldfields of Kalgoorlie-Boulder to the South Australia and the Northern Territory borders, is vast, isolated and rugged, dotted with towns as untamed as the countryside. It is a land of long, dusty red roads and big, bright night skies.

In 1893 Patrick 'Paddy' Hannan stumbled across gold near Kalgoorlie. His wasn't the first nor the only discovery – gold had been found the previous year at Coolgardie among other places – but the seam he discovered is the only one still being mined. In this barren landscape, many prospectors died before they even reached the goldfields, others lost their lives in the disease-ridden camps. Towns sprang up and died almost as quickly, as the gold dried up over the years.

Despite a population of more than 28,000, Kalgoorlie-Boulder still has the feel of a real frontier town. Tattooed locals are served by scantily clad waitresses (known as the 'skimpies') and gambling, brothels and Harley Davidsons are all in high demand. It is Australia's largest gold producer, and its wealth can be seen in the grand facades of its elegant public buildings. The Palace Hotel, with its opulent Victorian décor, features a continuous up-to-the-minute display of shares and gold prices on its outdoor walls.

Despite the town's remoteness, there is a massive demand for land and property in Kalgoorlie, far outstripping the supply. The miners of the outback are riding high on an economic boom.

The lonely Western Australian outback is also dotted with classic country pubs. In the Grand Hotel at Kookynie, you can still get full board for about $60 a day. On the Pilbara Coast, the pink, corrugated-roofed Whim Creek Pub once had a resident, beer-drinking camel, and is now believed to be haunted by a man killed there in a bar brawl in 1912.

At the **Argyle Diamond Mine** near Kununurra, in the East Kimberley region (main picture). Female drivers are highly sought after for their delicate touch with these expensive, specialist pieces of equipment.

Mustering the cattle at Digger's Rest station in the Kimberley (above).

SPORTFILE

There's nothing quite like Freo and the Weagles playing the western derby at Subi, is there? To the outsider, Western Australian sport appears to have a penchant for bizarre names. There's Subiaco Oval, for instance. Known as Subi, this is the home of the West Coast Eagles and Fremantle Dockers AFL teams, the Western Force rugby union franchise and, occasionally, the Wallabies.

Subiaco might pass as an Aboriginal name, but is in fact Italian. Home to the Nyungah people for about 50,000 years, the Perth suburb welcomed a group of Benedictine monks in 1851, who called their monastery New Subiaco after their old home town.

Then there's the 'Whacker', home ground of the Western Warriors cricket team and sometimes the Australian XI, and famed until recently for a bouncy pitch and sea breezes that gave batsmen nightmares and fast bowlers wet dreams. As any self-respecting cricket buff will explain, however, it is in fact spelled WACA and is an acronym for Western Australian Cricket Association.

That famous breeze also has a strange moniker of its own. The Fremantle Doctor is not a GP based in Perth's ocean port, but a wind that blows most afternoons off the Indian Ocean – the same wind that propelled John Bertrand's crew on *Australia II* to a momentous victory over the United States in the 1983 America's Cup yacht race.

It was the first time in 132 years that the United States had been beaten in the world's most famous sailing regatta, prompting Australia to erupt in celebration and a tipsy Prime Minister Bob Hawke to comment that any boss who sacked an employee for taking the next day off was 'a bum'.

The event also transformed Fremantle and ensured permanent places in sporting folklore for both the boxing kangaroo mascot and the unconventional 'winged keel' designed by the late boat builder Ben Lexcen.

ACTIVE LIVING

With seven out of ten Western Australians claiming to be involved in physical activity at least once a year, this is the **most active state**, statistically speaking, in Australia.

Others might suggest that these are just damned lies, but given the abundance of open space, warm weather and beautiful coastline in the Wildflower State, why woudn't Westralians be the outdoor types?

According to the Australian Bureau of Statistics, they're especially fond of water and wind-related pursuits, such as sailing and windsurfing, as well as cycling and swimming.

A windsurfer practises for the **Laneelin Ocean Classic**.

WHEN IN ...

... the Subi stands for a Dockers game:

Freo, way to go.
Hit 'em real hard,
Send them down below.
Freo give 'em the old heave-ho.
We are the Freo Dockers.

... the Subi stands watching the Eagles:

We're the Eagles ... West Coast Eagles,
And we're here to show you why.
We're the big birds. Kings of the big game.
We're the Eagles, we're flying high.

... the 'Bay of Glory' for A-League soccer:

Stuff 'em all, stuff 'em all,
The long and the short and the tall.
'Cos we are the Glory,
And we are the best.
We are the Glory,
So stuff all the rest.

A young **Fremantle Dockers** supporter shows his colours.

In recent years, it has been more than merely the names of western sporting events and venues that were unusual. More and more, it's the events and venues themselves.

In the Avon Descent whitewater race, teams and individuals paddle 134 kilometres of the Avon and Swan Rivers from Northam to Perth. Ouch. At the Gravity Games H_2O, held in Perth since 2004 – the first time a Gravity Games had been held outside the United States – the order of the day is extreme watersports such as wakeboarding, kitesurfing and tow-in surfing, as well as a few land-based extremes, such as skateboarding. But that's tame compared to the Red Bull Air Race series, which Perth hosted in 2006, where some of the world's top gun pilots had to navigate an obstacle course in the sky, in the fastest possible time.

And if you think regular sport in the west is wacky, wait until you see what they do when they're in a silly mood. At Lake Lefroy, these salty seadogs are so enamoured of sailing and yet so far from the ocean that they do it on dry land instead. The Sandgropers Land Yacht Club is based at Rockingham but gets together on the saltpan to ride the wind in purpose-built 'boats' with wheels attached.

In the Pilbara, all that time spent down a deep shaft looking for iron ore affects the miners so profoundly that, once a year, they load a heavy duty wheelbarrow full of iron ore and push it 120 kilometres from the Pub (the Whim Creek Hotel) to the Port (Hedland). They do, however, raise plenty of money for charity in the meantime, so nobody has ever questioned the wisdom of the Black Rock Stakes, as it's known.

THE SPORTING CALENDAR

Michael 'Chuck' Norris at the **Gravity Games H2O**.

JANUARY Give your neck a workout watching the **Hopman Cup**, one of the hottest tennis events on the circuit. And head to the historic WACA, to catch the **international and national cricket matches**.

APRIL The **AFL** season starts, and with it, the big question: can the mighty Weagles maintain their position with so much internal disruption? Head to the Subi to find out (oh, and to watch Fremantle).

MAY Do you like your sport rough or genteel? **The Battle of Bunbury** is a fixture of regional footy here; then there's the **Oceanique WA PGA Championship**, where Australian and international professional golfers vie for a prize.

AUGUST Whether you've got two or four wheels, the renowned **Australian Safari** is the ultimate off-road adventure with competitors tearing up 5000 km of gruelling outback terrain from Kununurra to Perth.

SEPTEMBER Spot a horse-racing celebrity (Damien Oliver, Lee Freedman – who said to take some Berocca) at **The Round**, a week-long event planned around three major race meetings, culminating with what's been called 'Australia's biggest party'.

OCTOBER If that wasn't enough horses for you, the **Kulin Bush Races** – in the heart of the wheatbelt – is made for families. Pack your swag, tent, caravan, ute … And if you think you're hard enough, take part in the **Mainpeak Collie Marathon Relay** (it only involves cycling, horse-riding, canoeing, swimming, mountain-biking and running).

NOVEMBER Well, it certainly gives these guys wings. The international **Red Bull Air Race**, with the Perth skyline and Swan River as its backdrop, has been dubbed motor racing in the sky – for good reason. Don't watch if you suffer from vertigo.

DECEMBER The water's where it's at. **The Gravity Games H₂O** is billed as the 'ultimate action sports, lifestyle and music festival'. And the crazy stunts and hot bodies don't end there … The Ironman Western Australia Triathlon shows off the state's natural beauty (and some seriously fit men and women).

ARTSANDCULTURE

Perhaps it is the sense of freedom, or the isolation and wildness of the country. Whatever it is, Western Australia seems to produce some unique and interesting art, literature and theatre.

The tradition began with ancient Aboriginal rock art. Murujuga, on the Coral Coast, is often considered to hold the largest collection of petroglyphs (rock carvings) in the world. Some are said to date back to the previous Ice Age, others show the thylacine (Tasmanian tiger), which became extinct on the mainland thousands of years ago. A little further south, the Kimberley is home to the Bradshaw paintings. Named after the first European to discover them in 1891, their style is unique amongst all Aboriginal rock painting.

The coveted work of contemporary Aboriginal artists can be seen all over Western Australia, in galleries such as the Maalinup in Perth and the Laverton Outback Gallery, which specialises in desert painters. Theatre troupes such as Yirra Yaakin Noongar, which is one of Australia's few Aboriginal-run performing companies, showcase indigenous theatre.

The coveted work of contemporary Aboriginal artists can be seen all over Western Australia, in galleries which specialise in desert painters.

There is also a strong tradition of European culture in the state. The stunning Edwardian-era His Majesty's Theatre in Perth features international acts as well as local ones, such as the Midnite Youth Theatre Company. The state also has its own opera company and symphony orchestra. WAAPA (the Western Australian Academy of Performing Arts), has a global reputation as a trainer of performers of all stripes. Its alumni include actors Hugh Jackman and William McInnes.

Lovers of popular culture are also catered for. Broome is home to Australia's oldest outdoor cinema, Sun Pictures, and the state boasts some of the country's best rock venues, such as the Newport in Fremantle and The Amplifier Bar in Perth.

Australian author Robert Drewe's recent bestselling memoir, *The Shark Net* (later adapted as a miniseries starring Tim Draxl, William McInnes, Angie Milliken and Dan Wyllie), is a beautifully evocative piece about growing up in Perth during the reign of one of Australia's most notorious serial killers: Erik Cooke, the last man hanged in the state. Drewe's childhood world of simple pleasures – pristine beaches, clear skies, trusting faces and small-town friendliness – is in stark contrast to this shocking event which helped shape the country's social consciousness.

Sun Pictures, now part of Sun Cinemas, opened in 1916 with the English racing drama *Kissing Cup*.

EST.1916

THE WORLDS OLDEST PICTURE GARDENS.

7.30p.m. START UNLESS STATED

Admission Adults $8
            Children $5
            Concession $6

ALEC BALDWIN   KIM BASINGER

The HOT The HANDLE

MONDAY
TUESDAY

· COMING SOON · COMING SOON · COMING SOON ·

SUNDAY
THURSDAY

SCHWARZENEGGER
TERMINATOR 2
JUDGMENT DAY

THE FESTIVAL CALENDAR

The state's isolation works in its favour, with Western Australia having a venerable, yet quirky, festival tradition, which keeps locals and visitors entertained.

Perth International Arts Festival created in 1953, this is the oldest celebration of international arts in Australia. The festival is financed by the state lottery, and every year it has a different theme – recently these have included 'Journey', 'Transcendence' and 'The Human Family'.

The Fremantle Street Art Festival thousands flock to the port city every Easter to see the world's best buskers, from countries as diverse as Canada, the USA, Portugal and the UK, including acts such as Hot Nuts and Popcorn, a comedy duo from Canada, and Spanna, an Australian clown.

Northbridge Festival Artrage, a contemporary art collective based in Perth, puts on this eclectic event, featuring the likes of street performers, fire and water displays, breakdancer battles and a pet photo booth.

PopEyed flex before their performance at the Fremantle Street Art Festival.

Batavia Celebrations every June Geraldton stages lectures, events and sometimes a concert to commemorate the shipwreck of the ill-fated *Batavia*, a Dutch ship which struck a reef off the Western Australian coast in 1629, with fatal consequences. By the time the crew was rescued, there had been a mutiny, and 120 of the survivors had been murdered.

Rock-It a rock music festival held twice a year at the Arena Joondalup in the northern suburbs of Perth. Recent acts have included Grinspoon, Silverchair and Powderfinger.

Blues at Bridgetown a popular blues festival with a three-day-long jambaroo which boasts 170 hours of music and a huge all-day street party.

Aboriginal artists from the Kimberley work on a giant collective canvas at Pike's Pirnini outstation in the northern fringes of the desert.

READ ... WATCH ... LISTEN TO ...

Tim Winton one of Australia's finest living novelists, known chiefly for *Cloudstreet*, which was made into a very successful play.

Randolph Stow born in Geraldton, Stow has written novels, poetry, operas and children's books, and won the Miles Franklin Award in 1958 for his novel, *To the Islands*.

Japanese Story set in the harsh landscape of the Pilbara, a geologist (played by Toni Collette) is stranded with a Japanese client she is reluctantly hosting. Love follows.

Rabbit Proof Fence the story of two young Aboriginal girls who, in 1931, ran away from school and followed the protective fence that crosses the state to find their home at Jigalong.

Last Train to Freo two ex-cons and a young female law student share the last train to Fremantle, when the guards are on strike.

Eskimo Joe won acclaim with the 2004 album, *A Song is a City*, which went double-platinum. The band have since released an even more successful album, *Black Fingernails, Red Wine*.

John Butler Trio a roots band led by John Butler, who was born in California but moved to WA when he was 11.

NATURALWONDERS

From the tropical north to the temperate south-west, Western Australia is blessed with incredible natural wonders in the form of gorges, lakes, waterfalls, reefs and flowers – lots and lots of flowers.

The rugged Kimberley is best seen by four-wheel drive, particularly to cover the 667 kilometres of the rough Gibb River Road. Dotted along this memorable route are huge, alien-like termite nests and distinctive, plump shapes of the boab tree. When the Kimberley is dry, it's hard to imagine it otherwise, but in its torrential wet season, it teems with lush greenery, tropical birds and crocodiles.

In a land of such contrasts, water has etched its indelible mark through the rock and dust. The Kimberley is gorge country. The colourful walls of Geike Gorge were once an ancient barrier reef. Windjana Gorge was carved, according to Aboriginal legend, by the massive Rainbow Serpent. And Bell Gorge features a spectacular cascade of pools, cliffs and ledges.

Just beyond the eastern end of the Gibb River Road, in the Purnululu National Park, is the maze of beehive-shaped rock formations known as the Bungle Bungles. This magical-looking terrain stretches for hundreds of kilometres of bulbous mounds, deep chasms and hidden tunnels. A particularly impressive part of the Bungles is the vast, dome-shaped Cathedral Gorge, which features a small lagoon at its bottom.

Stone and water also define Karijini, in the Pilbara. Here the deep-red rock has formed into jagged, stepped chasms and sinuous, water-rounded layers. Squeezing through tight gorges, inching along narrow ledges, wading through subterranean streams, swimming in crystal-clear pools … in Karijini you feel like you've found a lost world.

Elsewhere in the state, limestone has made its distinctive mark. North of Perth are The Pinnacles, a sea of bizarre pointed rocks, sticking up from the bright yellow sand dunes. And heading east is the world's largest single piece of limestone: the Nullarbor Plain. Derived from the Latin for 'no trees', the vast area is as featureless and arid as the moon. 'Crossing the Nullarbor' holds an almost mythical significance – it represents the true outback, in all its harshness.

The strange and **magnificent boab trees**, off the Gibb River Road (main picture).

An aerial shot of the **Bungle Bungles** (above).

In a land
of such
contrasts,
water has
etched its
indelible
mark through
the rock
and dust.

Prehistoric rock faults helped forge the spectacular **waterfall at Weano Gorge** in Karijini National Park in the Pilbara region.

MARINEMAGIC

Western Australia's marine environment is among the most pristine and biologically diverse in the world, and ranges from the warm, tropical waters and colourful coral off the Kimberley coast to the cool, temperate waters and sponge gardens of the Great Australian Bight. The state's coast is more than 13,500 kilometres long and makes up about 40 per cent of Australia's total shoreline.

Western Australia's Coral Coast is an incredible destination for the eco-tourist. Ningaloo Reef, Australia's 'other' great barrier reef, is literally jumping with marine life, from stingrays to whale

The friendly dolphins of **Monkey Mia**.

Twilight Beach, Esperance, is one of the most popular in the state.

LOCAL LEGENDS

Stromatolites are not the most interesting-looking of things, but they are ecologically important. These rocky masses, found in the salty waters of Hamelin Pool in Shark Bay, are covered in an algae-shaped microbe. At night the microbes fold over and trap calcium. By exuding sticky chemicals they constantly add new layers to their mass. They don't seem to lead very exciting lives, but without them we wouldn't be here. Their evolutionary history spans back to the dawn of life on earth, and they helped to oxygenate the planet so that we could evolve.

sharks. As Australia's largest 'fringing' reef, it lies much closer to shore than its famous Queensland counterpart. Its isolation from the rest of the country – and indeed, the world – means that many of its 200 species of coral are well-preserved, and divers here encounter limestone shelves, coral bommies, as well as countless schools of fish like snapper and coral trout. Whale sharks also travel past the reef and greenback turtles lay their eggs on the beaches. Humpback whales can be spotted off the coast in June and July.

South of Ningaloo Marine Park is the stunning UNESCO World Heritage site of Shark Bay. Its collection of peninsulas, islands and salty waters is not only beautiful but also of great zoological importance; it is home to about 10,000 dugongs who graze on the vast seagrass beds, as well as playful schools of bottlenose dolphins, some of whom are so sophisticated that they even use 'tools', protecting their beaks with a sponge while searching for food on the sea bottom. The area also supports more than 230 species of birds and about 150 species of reptiles, as well as being a breeding ground for many crustaceans, sharks and rays.

NATURE'S PLAYGROUND

Western Australia has a plethora of incredible wildlife. The sun-drenched Kimberley, for example, is a mecca for reptile lovers. Relatively harmless freshwater crocodiles lurk in the rivers and inlets, staying out of the way of the larger and more ferocious salties. Smaller, more manageable reptiles are also found here, such as goannas, little thorny devils and the spectacular frill-necked lizard.

WILDFLOWER WA

Western Australia is known as the **Wildflower State**, and a trip to the Midlands during spring will explain why. The normally red earth gives way to a carpet of red, yellow, purple, white and blue wildflowers; some believe it is the largest natural garden in the world. There are 12,000 wildflower species in the state, including kangaroo paws, banksias, orchids, cat's paws and smoke bushes.

In the north, wildflowers will appear in July and sometimes last until September. The Golden Outback and Coral Coast regions are known for their abundance of lollipop-shaped everlastings, but wattles, hakeas, dampiera, purple peas and Shark Bay daisies are common too. In the Pilbara area there are yellow native hibiscus, bluebells, sticky cassia, native fuchsias and many more.

Desert wildflowers of the **Pilbara**.

The towering **karri trees** of Warren National Park (main picture).

A couple of **cute quokkas** (inset).

The north is also the perfect spot for birdwatchers. An estimated 175,000 birds roost and feed in Broome's Roebuck Bay every year before returning to the Arctic to breed. More than 270 species have been observed here. Magpie geese and dozens of types of duck are prevalent in the north, as well as ibis, large cranes and the indigenous jabiru. Down south, fairy penguins are a favourite, living in the sand burrows and limestone caverns of Shoalwater Marine Park, near Perth.

Also living near Perth is an animal unique to the West. The quokka, which looks like a short, squat wallaby, is all but extinct on mainland Australia but survives on Rottnest Island, where there are no cats or foxes to hunt it. These friendly creatures also gave the island its name. In 1696 the explorer Willem de Vlamingh mistook them for rats and named the island 'Rottenest' – Dutch for 'rat nest'.

Perhaps unsurprisingly for such a vast state, Western Australia grows its trees big. The Valley of the Giants, in the state's south-west, is home to towering karri and tingle forests, which visitors can view from a tree-top walk, 38 metres above the ground. And if that isn't high enough for you, it's possible to climb some of the area's former fire-watching trees. The Gloucester Tree in Pemberton, for example, is 61 metres tall. The way up is on a series of well-spaced metal spikes set in a spiral around its trunk

SIGNS OF GOVERNMENT

Parliament House on North Terrace, Adelaide, was opened in 1939, but, due to ongoing financial constraints, it had to be built in several stages over 65 years.

On the **coat of arms**, the shield features a piping shrike. Above are Sturt's desert peas on a wreath of the state colours; below are symbols of agriculture and industry.

The **state's flag** is a blue background with a Union Jack and the state badge – the piping shrike.

NATURAL AMBASSADORS

First collected by William Dampier in the 17th century, the striking **Sturt's desert pea** is found all over South Australia.

The **hairy-nosed wombat**, a thick-set marsupial, is most abundant on Eyre Peninsula, the Gawler Ranges and the Nullarbor Plain.

The **piping shrike**, closely resembling a magpie, was known to be resourceful, daring and brave in defence of its nest. These were the qualities chosen to represent South Australia from 1901.

The **leafy seadragon**, an emblem since 2001, is a distinctive and spectacular relative of the seahorse. It is a protected species in South Australian waters.

PEOPLEFILE

There's a better class of person in South Australia. There always has been. The reason is simple, of course. Unlike the awful convict settlements that gave birth to Sydney, Hobart, Melbourne and Brisbane, Adelaide was established as a freely-settled, planned British province. No nasty crooks here, thank you very much. Not in the beginning, anyhow.

To this day, it is one of the most Anglo-Saxon of Australia's states. As the old joke goes, multiculturalism in South Australia is said to be in evidence when there are more brunettes than blondes in any given place.

They call South Australians 'croweaters' because early settlers were known to eat the meat of crows and other birds. But this doesn't seem to have held them back; croweaters punch well above their weight when it comes to producing extraordinary people.

Former Prime Minister Gough Whitlam once described Lord Howard Florey as 'easily the most important man born in Australia', – which would also make Florey one of the least recognised – for helping to bring the antibiotic penicillin to the world. Health experts now estimate that it has saved the lives of 50 million people.

The Festival State is also likely to give Australia its first saint. Mary MacKillop was born east of the border in Victoria, but it was in Penola, South Australia, that she established St Joseph's, the nation's first free Catholic school, in 1866. A year later she founded the Sisters of St Joseph of the Sacred Heart, the first religious order to be founded by an Australian. She was beatified in 1995.

Lowitja O'Donoghue is another woman from the south who has notched up a few firsts. In 1976 she was the first Aboriginal woman to be awarded an Order of Australia and she was Australian of the Year in 1984 for the work she has done for the welfare of her people.

Adelaide's Tim Flannery took that title in 2007, a year in which the warnings he had been giving Australians for years finally hit home. Al Gore's documentary *An Inconvenient Truth* was the movie that made climate change a mainstream issue, but Flannery's book *The Weather Makers* was the cause's Bible.

South Australia even gave the country an astronaut. Andy Thomas was selected by NASA in 1992 and has been to space several times, most memorably, and courageously, as part of the *Discovery* space shuttle's return to flight mission after 2003's *Columbia* disaster.

MOST LIKELY TO SAY:

I think I'll take an early minute.

The great white was THIS big.

Would you like to daahnce?

LEAST LIKELY TO SAY:

I can't find a church anywhere!

I really don't like red wine.

I reckon we have enough festivals.

Croweaters punch well above their weight when it comes to producing extraordinary people.

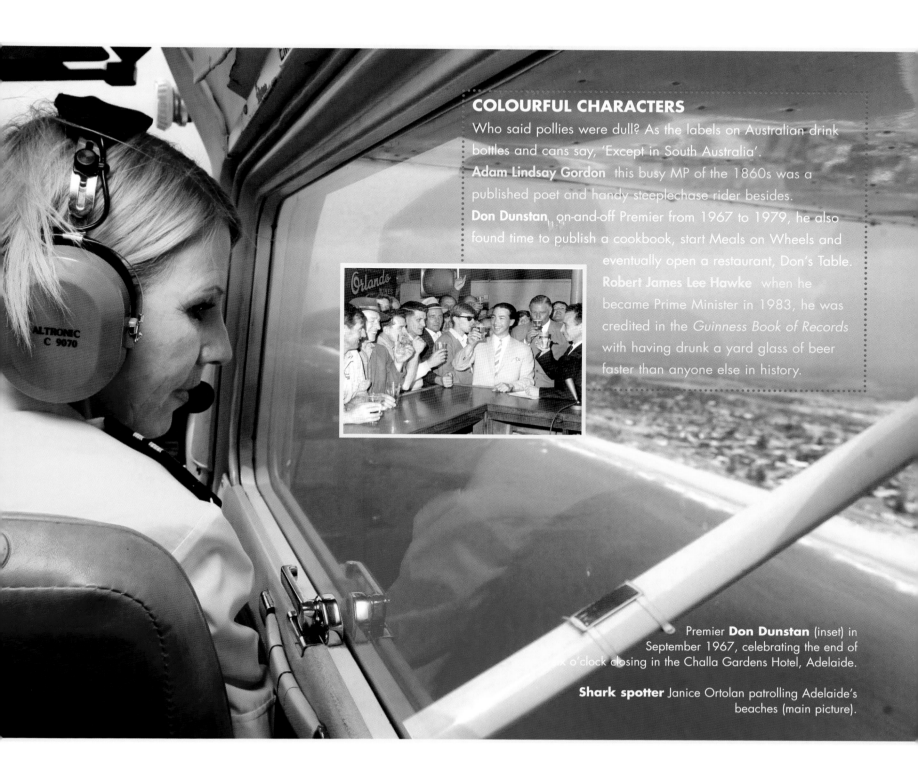

COLOURFUL CHARACTERS

Who said pollies were dull? As the labels on Australian drink bottles and cans say, 'Except in South Australia'.

Adam Lindsay Gordon this busy MP of the 1860s was a published poet and handy steeplechase rider besides.

Don Dunstan on-and-off Premier from 1967 to 1979, he also found time to publish a cookbook, start Meals on Wheels and eventually open a restaurant, Don's Table.

Robert James Lee Hawke when he became Prime Minister in 1983, he was credited in the *Guinness Book of Records* with having drunk a yard glass of beer faster than anyone else in history.

Premier **Don Dunstan** (inset) in September 1967, celebrating the end of six o'clock closing in the Challa Gardens Hotel, Adelaide.

Shark spotter Janice Ortolan patrolling Adelaide's beaches (main picture).

CITYSTYLE

It was not only the state that was fastidiously planned from the get-go. Its main city, Adelaide, was very carefully designed by Colonel William Light, the state's first surveyor-general, in 1836. To ensure it would never grow beyond a comfortable size, he placed parks on four sides of the two major centres, Adelaide and North Adelaide, creating what looked like a square figure eight. The CBD is a neat grid of wide streets that can be traversed in half an hour.

Colonel Light was criticised for putting the city too far from the sea, but boldly declared: 'I leave it to posterity … to decide whether I am entitled to praise or to blame.' Today he can be found in statue form on Montefiore Hill, overlooking his masterpiece of urban planning – and pointing at it victoriously.

The River Torrens flows through the city and was made to look more impressive than it really is by being dammed. On one side of town, Gulf St Vincent stretches away from the beach at Glenelg towards the great Southern Ocean. On the other, the Mount Lofty Ranges hem in Australia's neatest capital city, which was named after King William IV's wife, Queen Adelaide.

About the only thing the planners didn't get right was the water. Being the driest city in the driest state on the globe's driest continent and relying in part on the ever drier Murray River for supply doesn't make good drinking water easy to come by. Some jokers say that's why Bickford's Lime Cordial, a South Australian icon, became so popular.

Maybe it's also why the state makes arguably the best wine and beer in the country …

DID YOU KNOW?

Adelaide is Australia's undisputed home of **speechless TV animals**. It was here in the 1960s that a pantless bear first appeared on the box. He was called 'B Bear' until a competition was held to find a new name and 'Humphrey' was the winning entry. Humphrey B Bear is still on TV today.

Fat Cat, however, is not. The large marmalade-coloured feline, also an Adelaidian, was cruelly axed in 1992.

Australia's neatest capital city, which was named after King William IV's wife, Queen Adelaide.

A BROAD CHURCH

In 1976, a **clairvoyant housepainter** predicted that an earthquake and tidal wave would destroy the usually pious Adelaide to punish it for turning into a 'sin city'. He even named the date: 19 January.

On the morning of the 19th, after some families had gone so far as to do a runner from the South Australian capital, then-Premier Don Dunstan went to the seaside at Glenelg with a horde of fellow disbelievers and watched as ... nothing happened.

So maybe God doesn't mind Adelaide so much after all.

Adelaide's glam set are to be found at funky haunts such as **Moskva Vodka Bar** in Hindley Street (opposite, above).

Da Klinic (opposite, below), an underground shop with a mini skate ramp, break room, DJs, hip-hop workshops and skater gear.

St Peter's Cathedral (left) in front of the city's newer buildings.

BEACHLIVING

When he was looking to found a city, Governor Hindmarsh walked directly inland from the sea, to the flat plains on which Adelaide now stands. That same route is followed today by Adelaide's tram – its only tram – which chugs and dings from the city centre to the seaside suburb of Glenelg.

Glenelg (inset) at the end of the vintage tram line from the city has a bustling café strip leading to a lovely swimming beach.

Sky House (main picture) at LifeTime private retreats on Kangaroo Island.

Cosmopolitan Adelaidians now travel a little further afield for a weekend break by the coast, heading to the seaside villages and holiday spots of the Yorke and Fleurieu peninsulas, the Coorong or the Murray riverlands.

South Australia has 3700 kilometres of coast, with a variety of seascapes from peaceful harbours and pristine beaches to ragged cliffs and pounding surf. Compared to the eastern states, it is largely undeveloped and, well, rather English.

An influx of Cornish miners when copper was found on the Yorke Peninsula in 1861 led to the area being dubbed 'Australia's Little Cornwall' after the south-western tip of England. And in the past this area resembled Cornwall for all the wrong reasons. Where the English original was the setting for the pirate tales of Robert Louis Stevenson, the Australian version gained thriving whaling, sealing and smuggling industries.

Today, mining has moved on from the Yorke, and fishing, agriculture and tourism are the mainstays of the local economy, attracting visitors to its great surfing and diving spots.

There are further reminders of the 'mother country' in towns such as Beachport, where a 772-metre jetty points out from the former whaling station into the Great Australian Bight.

Many think Goolwa is the southern coastline's prettiest beach, but it was pipped by a South Australian cousin at Vivonne Bay, Kangaroo Island, in a 2003 poll.

SEASCAPES: THE VICTOR HARBOR HORSE-DRAWN TRAM

When a train line opened between Adelaide and Goolwa in the 1880s, **Victor Harbor** became a favourite spot for holidays, particularly honeymoons. Taking the horse-drawn tram across the timber causeway, out to Granite Island, became a much cherished ritual, captured by Madelaine Brunato in her poem 'The Horses': 'But the highlight of all their visits / that they carry down memory lane / is the ride on the tram with a clip-clip-clop / and a toss of the noble mane.'

COUNTRYSTYLE

While some country towns in the eastern states struggle to remain viable, South Australia's bush is alive with agriculture and industry, from wine to wheat, wool and mining. And it looks as though they'll continue to thrive, as long as the rain arrives from time to time.

Many of the state's towns are historically charming, such as the Lutheran-built Tanunda and Hahndorf, with its art academy inspired by former resident and celebrated artist Sir Hans Heysen. When Heysen first took to painting landscapes, says the *Australian Dictionary of Biography*, 'he developed a deep love of the Adelaide

THE DOG FENCE

Thanks to Phillip Noyce's film, *Rabbit Proof Fence*, moviegoers now know of the two rabbit fences that cross Australia – but few know of the **dog fence** stretching 5400 kilometres from the Great Australian Bight through South Australia and NSW to the bleak scrub country of Queensland's Bunya Mountains.

It divides the continent between cattle country on one side and sheep country on the other, the latter needing protection from the hungry native dingoes that roam the interior.

It requires constant maintenance. In 2007 the ABC reported that excitable bull camels were knocking holes in the fence to get to females who were on heat on the other side.

Cattle graze by the studio of **Hans Heysen's house**, 'The Cedars'.

Hills, tramping about with his paintbox and stool whenever he could'. He grew to love the Onkaparinga Valley near the villages of Hahndorf and Grunthal, and it features in many of his early works.

Some towns along the Murray River, even their residents might be surprised to know, began life as communist outposts in the 1890s, when unemployment in Adelaide was at an all-time high and jobless people headed out to the country to establish villages based on red principles. These societies failed mostly because the city communists were lousy farmers or missed Adelaide and decided to return. But some villages survived, such as Waikerie, which has a blossoming of citrus orchards.

As in country areas all over Australia, the state pulls its weight when it comes to building Big Things; there's the Biggest Rocking Horse in the World at Gumeracha in the Adelaide Hills, the Big Crayfish at Kingston in the south-east, the Big Galah at Kimba and the Big Orange at Berri.

South Australia's vast outback is also home to the world's largest farm. At more than 30,000 square kilometres, Anna Creek Station is bigger than Belgium. Its 20 or so residents are not the only lonely ones in the state. Cook, a former support town for the Indian-Pacific railway and now the only stop between Kalgoorlie and Adelaide, has a population of four, while a former railway employee called Ziggy now lives alone near the track at Barton, which is pretty much the middle of nowhere. He does at least have his 12 dogs for company – they're all called Dog.

But perhaps the most unusual and best known of South Australia's country towns is Coober Pedy, the hub of Australia's lucrative opal-mining industry. Here summer temperatures regularly climb over 40 degrees Celsius, so the miners live beneath the ground like moles in their surprisingly comfortable dug-out homes. Even Coober Pedy's church and golf course are underground.

The town's name is said to come from the Aboriginal words *kupa piti*, meaning 'white man in a hole', which, while it might describe how the townsfolk now live, was first used with reference to their tendency to dig for gems.

An underground living room in **Coober Pedy**.

The town of Willunga holds an **Almond Blossom Festival** every July.

A TASTE OF THE COUNTRY

Sheep milk cheeses from Island Pure

Goolwa mussels

Self-caught trout from Tooperang

Coffin Bay oysters

Mt Compass venison

Organic Ligurian honey from Kangaroo Island

Swan Almonds

Menz FruChocs

Golden North Ice Cream

Farmers Union Iced Coffee

Pick your own at the **Beerenberg Strawberry Farm** near Hahndorf.

Driving into South Australia on a major highway, visitors are often surprised to be stopped and searched. But it's not the usual sort of contraband that will land them in trouble with the South Australian authorities — it's their fruit.

As the only state in Australia that is certified 'fruit fly free' and the heart and soul of the country's grape- and citrus-growing industries, South Australia is particularly choosy about what it allows to be carried across the border. As the *saculture.com* website jokes, 'A fruit fly outbreak spells disaster for both the South Australian fruit industry and local newsreaders, who are compelled to repeat the phrase "fruit fly free" numerous times.'

The state's carefully protected fruit orchards are the foundation of its many distinctive fruit-based food brands. Beerenberg Farm in Hahndorf makes jams, condiments and marmalades that find their way into the pantries of gourmands throughout Australia and 22 other countries. What began as a batch of strawberry jam to get rid of a glut of fruit in 1971 is now served up in 300 of the best hotels in the Asia-Pacific region. And if you think that you already know which is your favourite brand of tomato sauce but you haven't yet tried theirs, think again.

There are more delights to be found off the mainland too. Kangaroo Island is thought to be the only place in the world where a pure strain of the placid Ligurian bee exists, and this is where you'll find some of the best honey you ever tasted. The island also produces more olfactory pleasures, with a lavender farm at Emu Bay and the state's only commercial eucalyptus distillery at Emu Ridge.

Back on the mainland, in the mid north of the state, Golden North is South Australia's only ice cream producer and the only independent mainstream ice creamery in Australia. It makes a mean honey ice cream to go with its famous Giant Twins: slabs of vanilla, vanilla-choc or vanilla-strawberry ice cream smothered in chocolate.

PICKOFTHEVINE

'A concoction of wild fruits and sundry berries with crushed ants predominating,' is how one sceptical critic described the first ever vintage of Penfold's Grange Hermitage.

Little did he know, it was actually the second vintage he was tasting. The first had not even been exposed to critics because the maverick winemaker Max Schubert suspected they would not like it.

But palates have changed so much since that first tasting in the 1950s – when most Australians drank sherry – that a bottle of that first, secret 1951 batch recently sold for more than $52,000.

Penfold's Grange has now been declared a Heritage Icon by the National Trust of South Australia and has won more than 300 awards around the world. It is universally recognised as one of the world's best drops, and it is fitting that it comes from South Australia, the powerhouse of the Aussie wine industry.

Not only does South Australia produce most of the nation's plonk, but it boasts some of the oldest individual vines in the world, because the isolated Barossa Valley and Adelaide Hills managed to survive the great phylloxera plagues that wiped out vines across North America, Europe and Australia's east.

The state has a variety of what the French and the more articulate wine buffs call 'terroirs', from the relatively warm

Barossa, to the maritime McLaren Vale and Langhorne Creek regions, to the cooler Adelaide Hills, the picturesque Clare Valley and the 'terra rossa' soils on top of limestone in the Coonawarra region.

But the state's great strength in wine is its history, which dates back to the 1850s, when German and Silesian immigrants began planting in places such as the Barossa. The accumulated knowledge of those centuries has not only made South Australian wine the best on the whole, but has given the industry the confidence to become the most innovative in Australia.

'What's happening today is what's always happened in the Barossa,' Bob McLean, former owner of St Hallett, has said. 'People who've worked at the big successful companies are putting out their own wines, and as always, you better watch them.'

The website *winefront.com.au* says two of the current hotspots are in the south around Lyndoch, where Dutschke and Burge Family Winemakers in particular are producing fabulous wines, and in the Marananga/Seppeltsfield areas, where Two Hands, Torbreck, Barossa Valley Estate and Whistler have all recently set up cellar doors. 'They are new names, but they are of the same cloth, utilising the same old vines – the old is built into the new.'

One of the first: a bottle of **1951 Penfolds Grange Hermitage**.

Winemaker Ben Riggs at his McLaren Vale vineyard. His Mr Riggs Shiraz has been hailed as 'the new Grange'.

Banrock Station
Barossa Valley Estate
Chain of Ponds
d'Arenberg
Grosset
Hardy's
Henschke
Jacob's Creek
Katnook Estate
Mawson Ridge
Petaluma
Pewsey Vale
Rosemount Estate
Tatachilla
Wendouree
Yalumba

WINE ON WHEELS

To temper the effects of wine-tasting, visitors to the Clare Valley north of Adelaide intersperse each world-class glass of riesling with cycling a leg of the **Clare Valley Riesling Trail**, a 27-kilometre sealed trail that links the villages of the valley, its varied landscapes and its cellar doors.

SPORTFILE

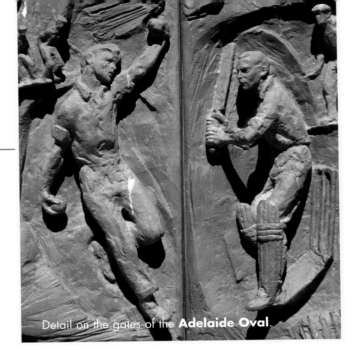

Detail on the gates of the **Adelaide Oval**.

Cricket aficionados have been known to say that the Adelaide Oval is one of the most picturesque and pleasant places to play or watch the gentleman's game. The place is so well kept that its curator, Les Burdett, is a household name.

Brett Richardson with his partner, triple Olympian Julien Prosser, practise their **beach volleyball**.

The Chappell brothers cut their teeth at the Adelaide Oval with the Southern Redbacks, as did David Hookes and Jason Gillespie. It also has a magical ability to provide Australia with its greatest cricketing moments, such as: Donald Bradman's 299 not out in 1931–32 against South Africa, which is the highest Test score ever; Craig McDermott's dodgy dismissal to lose by one run to the visiting West Indies in 1992–93; and Australia's defeat of England in the second Ashes test in 2006–07, which captain Ricky Ponting said was the best game he had ever played in.

AN ACTIVE LIFE

South Australians don't just enjoy watching the footy; they like to play it too. About 2.2 per cent of adults say they participate in Aussie rules, making South Australia the most active footy playing state in the country, according to the Australian Bureau of Statistics.

And croweating women are an active bunch also. Apparently two-thirds of them participate in sports, putting them second only to the women of the west in national terms, and making South Australia one of the few states in which the women are more sporty than the men. Go girls.

As for sports attendance, South Australians are the nation's most enthusiastic spectators of basketball (with 3 per cent of them watching a game each year) and motor sports (14 per cent), which is probably due to the concentration of people in Adelaide and the way in which the annual Clipsal 500 event takes over the capital city; in February, you can't walk down the street without tripping over a V8 Supercar.

But if the Oval is Adelaide's sporting wife, AAMI Stadium is the city's sporting mistress. A two-team town in the winter, Adelaide all but requires its citizens to have stamped on their birth certificate which Aussie Rules club they support, Port Adelaide Power or the Adelaide Crows.

Port was for many years the biggest, strongest club in the South Australian National Football League, but since the Crows joined the AFL first, in 1991, they now boast the biggest membership base in the country at about 50,000 one-eyed fans. They have never lost a Grand Final when they've made it to the big one and they've done that, on average, every five years.

In fact, as residents of the nation's fourth most populous state, croweaters excel in most national sporting competitions. Their basketballers, the Adelaide 36ers, have won four championships in 20 years, while their soccer team, Adelaide United, made it to the second A-League Grand Final in 2006–07.

ARTSANDCULTURE

The satirist Max Gillies, whose impersonation of former Prime Minister Bob Hawke is probably his best known, also does a great send-up of that species – most prevalent of all our cities in Adelaide – the culture vulture.

Gillies' Adelaidian character is a fellow with a plum in the mouth, a pink shirt and cravat, who speaks of 'things cultural' in a restaurant while sipping a glass of white wine. In some ways, he's not far off the mark.

Spoiled by the above-average investment of the state's governments in 'things cultural', croweaters have developed a keen critical sense over the years. From public artworks such as the metal spheres in Rundle Street – naughtily nicknamed 'Don's Balls' after Don Dunstan, the premier most responsible for promoting the arts down south – to the crafts at the Jam Factory (also a Dunstan initiative) or the Adelaide Symphony and Youth orchestras, they have more than their fair share of art to gaze at and dissect.

Maybe it was always that way. The rock art of the Flinders Ranges shows that culture in South Australia didn't begin with Don Dunstan, as does the impressive collection of Aboriginal artefacts at the South Australian Museum on North Terrace.

These days the heart of culture here is the Festival Centre, on the banks of the River Torrens, with its three theatres, an outdoor amphitheatre and a year-round program that peaks with the city's long and diverse list of festivals.

The terrace at the **Adelaide Festival Centre** (main picture), a key performing arts venue.

An indigenous **mural** (inset) on the walls of the Festival Centre.

Meanwhile, in the outside world, it's probably the state's films that have received the most attention. From the 1970s to the late '90s, the vibrant South Australian Film Corporation was responsible for making some of the country's best ever films. Remember Jack Thompson in *Sunday Too Far Away*, a movie about sheep and shearers? Or *Storm Boy* and *Blue Fin*, based on the novels of local author Colin Thiele and starring Greg Rowe and David Gulpilil?

More recently, director Rolf de Heer, who won acclaim for *Ten Canoes*, has kept the tradition alive, while the director Scott Hicks and the actor Geoffrey Rush launched their Hollywood careers here with *Shine*.

READ ... WATCH ... LISTEN TO ...

The Dog Fence James Woodford's compelling account of the 5400-kilometre fence that keeps out the dingoes.

All Things Bright and Beautiful Susan Mitchell's story of the Snowtown murders focuses on Adelaide's addiction to perfection.

Shine the 1996 Adelaide film about the pianist David Helfgott.

Breaker Morant anyone who has endured a history class about the Boer War has seen this. It was filmed in Burra, South Australia.

Pitch Black and Mad Max III Coober Pedy, Lunar Plains and Moon Plains provided the otherworldly settings for these sci-fi adventures.

Ben Folds the US musician, who wrote the song 'Adelaide', moved here and married a local girl.

'South Australia' a sea shanty, originally sung by wool traders en route to London, was made famous in the 1980s by The Pogues.

THEFESTIVALSTATE

Acrobat Letizia Cirri in *Il Cielo Che Danza* (The Dancing Sky) at the **Adelaide Festival of Arts** 2006.

They call it the Festival State for a very good reason; South Australia has pioneered the art of the festival down under and remains, pound for pound, the best place in the country to see, hear and drink in top quality, cutting-edge performances.

The big one, the Adelaide Festival of Arts, only happens every two years but is considered Australia's best by those in the know, partly because the city, with its cafés, restaurants, pubs and intimate, within-walking-distance venues, is just so made for it. Begun in 1960 and inspired by the Edinburgh Festival in Scotland, it is, in fact, a number of separate events held at the same time, incorporating opera, theatre, dance, music, cabaret and new media.

Among the satellite events are Adelaide Writers' Week, the world's largest literary festival; WOMADelaide, a world music festival; the Adelaide Festival of Ideas, an internationally respected talkfest; and the Adelaide Fringe Festival, for those whose tastes are a little less mainstream.

Directors of the Festival of Arts have included legends such as Robert Helpmann, Jim Sharman and Peter Sellars, and it is also an economic goldmine for the state. In 2006, for example, it used 29 indoor and outdoor venues, attracted 546,000 spectators, made an estimated $13.1 million and brought an estimated 11,100 people to South Australia from overseas, interstate and regional SA.

But the festival scene has spread way beyond the main event over the years – that's now just the biggest jewel in a festival crown. Here are just a few of the others on the calendar:

Markus Orchard with papier mâché friends at **WOMADelaide** (above). The Adelaide Cabaret Festival production of *Leading Ladies* (right).

The Barossa Music Festival classical intoxication for the ears among the vines of South Australia's first wine-growing region. There's also the Barossa Jazz Weekend, Barossa Under the Stars and Barossa Vintage Festival, with its olde-worlde maypoles, tug-o-war and brass bands.

The Adelaide Film Festival held in alternating years with the main festival, this one celebrates the state's filmmaking heritage.

Come Out a festival for children and young people in which they can create or experience artistic works.

The Adelaide Cabaret Festival takes in everything from show tunes to comic bands.

The South Australia Living Artists Festival this is the annual visual arts event, and it's entirely free!

The Jazz Festival for hipsters and groovy cats.

The Royal Adelaide Show for kids and the country cousins.

The Feast Festival a celebration of lesbian and gay culture.

The South Australian Country Music Festival held in Barmera each year, this recognises the best of, as they say, 'both types of music: country *and* western'.

NATURAL WONDERS

South Australia is a state of great contrasts. As the most arid state in Australia, its scenery does not have the lushness of Queensland or the pretty charm of Tasmania. But it does have plentiful wildlife and spectacular coastlines. Even its dryness – it has even more semi-desert than Western Australia – has its own peculiar beauty.

Not just a treeless plain, the Nullarbor National Park's 2,873,000 hectares protect part of the world's largest semi-arid karst landscape, layers of dissolved bedrock, which occasionally collapse into sinkholes, revealing underground caverns. The park is also home to the country's largest population of southern hairy-nosed wombats.

In the north of the state, the rugged purple folds of the Flinders Ranges are steeped in Aboriginal legend. More recently they have inspired artists and bushwalkers alike. The Heysen Trail ends here, in Parachilna Gorge, after its 1200-kilometre ramble from the Fleurieu Peninsula.

Walking trails also criss-cross the Murraylands to the south. The unique mallee shrublands and sand dunes of Karte Conservation Park are a favourite. They provide a habitat for the threatened mallee fowl, the endangered western whipbird and a number of rare orchids.

In Mount Gambier, in the state's south-east, a dormant maar volcano contains a huge crater lake. The 90-metre-deep waters of the stunning Blue Lake mysteriously turn an intense sapphire colour every summer. Legend says that a blue 'boonyip' stains the water when he rises from the bottom of the crater to greet the sun.

Dramatic Elder Range in the **Flinders Ranges** (main picture).

The fossil-rich depths of the **Naracoorte Caves** (inset, opposite).

Grass trees (or Black Boys) in **Para Wirra National Park** (right).

In the north of the state, the rugged purple folds of the Flinders Ranges are steeped in Aboriginal legend.

Beautiful rippling kelp gardens are home to strange sea creatures.

Where the plains meet the sea; dramatic cliffs of the **Great Australian Bight**.

GREATAUSTRALIANBITES

The **great white shark** (*Carcharodon carcharias*) is the world's largest predatory fish. It can grow up to 6 metres or more in length but looms larger in our collective psyche. Also known as a white pointer or, better still, 'white death', its teeth can be about 7.5 centimetres long, and millions of years of evolution have turned it into a fearsome hunter, capable of impressive bursts of speed – up to 40 kilometres per hour. The great white is a curious creatures and prone to taking test bites; in more than half of all known attacks, it has taken one bite and swum away. There have actually been only 64 fatal great white attacks in the past 130 years, 27 of which were in Australia. In that time, more people have actually been killed by domestic livestock, such as pigs.

Appropriately, you do find lots of great whites in the Great Australian Bight.

The state's coast is a big drawcard for locals and tourists alike. It boasts fairytale beaches of crystal blue water and soft white sand. And then there's the sweeping arc of the Great Australian Bight, which from the air looks remarkably like its homonym – a 'bite' taken out of the southern shore of Australia.

Offshore, things are just as interesting. The warm Leeuwin current flows into the Bight where it prevents cooler, nutrient-rich water from welling up from the deep, making these some of the least fertile seas in the world. Other temperate waters contain huge numbers of fish, birds and mammals, but the Great Australian Bight is different. An incredible diversity of endemism (meaning 'nowhere else in the world') has developed unique solutions to surviving in a place where food is in such short supply. Beautiful rippling kelp gardens are home to strange sea creatures. Delicate coloured sea dragons waft in and out of the seaweed like will-o'-the-wisps and cuttlefish mesmerise their victims with startling light displays.

Of course, one of the first things that comes to mind when South Australian waters are mentioned is the chilling great white shark. But it's not all scary – at places such as Baird Bay on the Eyre Peninsula, swimmers often have to share the waters with sea lions and dolphins; every year from June to October, whales and their calves swim to the Head of Bight on the Eyre Peninsula; and there is a colony of about 1000 little penguins on Granite Island.

KANGAROOISLAND

Blooms of a **Banksia ornata**, which is indigenous to the state.

Lazing on a beach, **sea lion** style.

Frisky **koalas receive contraceptive implants**, as their rising population threatens food resources.

The aptly named **Remarkable Rocks**, on Kangaroo Island's south coast, look more like a Picasso print than rock formations.

There is incredible wildlife all over South Australia – from the abundant flora and fauna of the Murray, to the bird breeding colony of The Coorong, home to the largest breeding colony of Australian pelicans and 238 other bird species. However, Kangaroo Island holds a special place in the state as a natural wildlife sanctuary.

Kangaroo Island separated from the mainland about 9500 years ago, and since then it has enjoyed an interesting human history, operating as an sealing and whaling colony during the early 19th century, as well as a home to escaped convicts and runaway soldiers.

For native wildlife, however, its isolation from the mainland has kept it free of introduced predators and pests, such as dingoes, rabbits and foxes. One third of the island is protected as conservation and national parks, and half the island has never been cleared of native vegetation. All native animals on the island are officially termed 'precious and protected'. So pristine is the environment that animals endangered on the mainland, such as koalas and the platypus, have been introduced here to boost their numbers.

Flinders Chase National Park comprises 33,000 hectares of spectacular wilderness and is home to large numbers of the island's native animals, including the Kangaroo Island kangaroo, the tammar wallaby, the short-beaked echidna and the southern brown bandicoot. About 5 per cent of all Australian sea lions call Kangaroo Island their home, and New Zealand fur seals are plentiful. They're a delight to watch, as they laze in the sun, hop lumpenly along the beach or bodysurf and dive joyfully in the waves.

Perched as it is on the edge of the continent, Tasmania is easy to overlook. But on closer inspection it's immediately obvious how interesting and appealing a state it is. With its fascinating history and gastronomic delights, not to mention the absolute magnificence of its natural forests, lakes, gorges and rivers, Tasmania may be small, but it is definitely perfectly formed.

Visitors on a ghost tour at **Port Arthur**.

STATEFILE

Tasmania was created about 12,000 years ago when the ice caps melted and the seas rose to separate the island from mainland Australia. Aboriginal people had been living in the region for over 23,000 years before their isolation from mainland indigenous communities.

Europeans arrived much later – the first reported sighting of the island was on 24 November 1642 by the Dutch explorer Abel Tasman. He gave the island the convoluted name of Anthoonij van Diemenslandt, but it was later shortened by the British to Van Diemen's Land.

In 1803 the British were worried that the French would gain a foothold on the island and exploit the whaling and timber resources in the south, so they established a penal colony at Risdon Cove on the eastern bank of the Derwent estuary. This was later abandoned for an alternative site five kilometres to the south, at Sullivans Cove, where fresh water was more plentiful. This settlement became known as Hobart Town, after Lord Hobart, the British Colonial Secretary of the time.

An 1857 painting by Henry Gritten, showing the **emerging Hobart Town**.

DID YOU KNOW?

In 1936 the last known **Tasmanian tiger** (*thylacine*) died at Hobart's Beaumaris Zoo. There have been reported sightings of the animal since then, but none has been confirmed.

The **first telephone call** in Australia was made in Tasmania, between Launceston and Campbell Town, in 1874.

Tasmania was the first Australian state to introduce a **compulsory state education** system in 1868.

VITAL STATISTICS

NICKNAMES:	the Apple Isle, the Holiday Isle
AREA:	90,758 km² (7th)
POPULATION:	489,000 (6th)
POPULATION DENSITY:	7.16 people per km² (4th)
LANDMARKS:	Port Arthur Prison, Cradle Mountain, Wineglass Bay, Richmond Bridge, Cataract Gorge, Macquarie Island, Franklin River, Lake Pedder
INDUSTRIES:	mining (including copper, zinc, tin, and iron), agriculture, forestry, tourism, hydro-electricity
SPORTS:	Aussie Rules, cricket, bushwalking
NATIONAL PARKS:	19, including Franklin–Gordon Wild Rivers, South West, Freycinet, Cradle Mt–Lake St Clair, Walls of Jerusalem
WORLD HERITAGE SITES:	Tasmanian Wilderness and Macquarie Island

The view down **Elizabeth Street** from the old Union Bank.

The early settlers were almost all convicts and their military guards, and they fanned out to form several penal colonies across the island, including Port Arthur in the south-east and Macquarie Harbour on the west coast. It soon gained a reputation as Australia's harshest penal colony, a place all convicts feared because of its isolation and ruggedness.

In 1825 Van Diemen's Land was made independent from New South Wales, with its own courts and Legislative Council. However, as more free settlers arrived, they grew increasingly unhappy with the convict presence, and after some lobbying, the transportation of convicts was stopped in 1853. To cut ties with what was regarded as an undesirable past, the colony was renamed after Abel Tasman, and in 1901 it became a state in the newly federated Commonwealth of Australia.

During the 1930s Depression the first hydro-electric schemes in Australia were built in Tasmania's Central Highlands, bringing a much-needed boost to the state's economy. This growth continued into the 1940s, when the mining and forestry industries also developed. These flourishing industries provided opportunities for the many migrants who arrived in the post-World War II immigration boom.

In the 1960s and '70s, Tasmania saw the birth of one of the world's first Green movements, as conservation groups responded to the encroachment of industry on the state's magnificent wilderness areas. The Tasmanian environment was spotlighted again in the 1980s, with widespread opposition to the Franklin River dam. It proved a major factor in the 1983 election of Bob Hawke as Prime Minister, and construction of the dam was halted in that same year.

TASMANIATODAY

Tasmania's island status has had a major influence on its development. Unlike other states, Tasmania never had a gold rush. Its lack of infrastructure and foreign investment, combined with a small population, further hampered its growth. But things have turned around for the Apple Isle.

Since the emergence of the conservation movement in the 1960s and '70s, Tasmanians have realised the incredible wealth of wilderness they have at their doorstep. A whopping 40 per cent of Tasmania is dedicated to reserves, national parks and World Heritage sites. The state is promoted as 'the Natural State' and the 'Island of Rejuvenation', and the introduction of the Spirit of Tasmania ferries (which now only cover the Devonport to Melbourne route) has enabled the tourist economy to flourish. Nowadays Tasmania has more visitors per year than its entire population. Perhaps the most amazing thing about Tasmania is that it has taken others so long to discover it.

Although relatively unpopulated compared to the rest of Australia, the property market here is flourishing. As on the mainland, the majority of the population sticks to the coast – in particular the north and south-east coasts, where the country is rich and fertile.

Tasmania also enjoys one of the country's best climates. Summers are mild and winters are tempered by the ubiquitous presence of the sea. Apart from tourism, the state's economy also relies on the mining and logging industries, as well as food exporting sectors – particularly its delicious seafood, such as Atlantic salmon, abalone and crayfish.

Mist hangs heavy over the atmospheric **Wielangta Forest**.

A whopping 40 per cent of Tasmania is dedicated to reserves, national parks and World Heritage sites.

THEGOODLIFE

A temperate climate, reliable rains and clean oceans mean Tasmania is rich in natural produce, from its seafood to its award-winning wines and exotic niche products like emu steaks, mutton birds, saffron, wakame seaweed and wasabi. Tasmania earns more than $440 million a year in food and beverage exports.

The fishing industry is concentrated in the east, around places such as Bicheno, where locals buy seafood straight off the boats; St Helen's, the largest fishing port; and Kettering, known for its oyster restaurants. Visitors to the island shouldn't miss its rock lobster, farmed Atlantic salmon, ocean trout and scallops. The booming abalone industry supplies more than a quarter of the world's fresh market.

The Huon Valley is the apple-growing region, and come summertime it offers the pick of delicious berries as well. The area's rolling pastures also produce delicious dairy products, especially blues and bries, cheddars and camemberts. But the north-west is perhaps the epicentre of Tasmanian cheese-making, with the likes of Mount Roland Cheese, Lacrum Dairy Farm and King Island Dairies.

Tasmania produces plenty of drink to go with all that food: James Boag's beer from Launceston, whisky from the Hellyers Road Distillery in Burnie and the wines of Tamar Valley, Home Hill and Pipers River. Although the wine industry isn't a large one, it is distinguished, specialising in cold climate varieties such as champagne, rieslings and gewurztraminers, chardonnays and pinot noirs.

With such a wide variety of food, Tasmanians love to celebrate it. There's the Chocolate Winterfest in Latrobe, the Agfest, the Royal Hobart Show, the Royal Launceston Show and the Taste of Tasmania, timed to coincide with the Sydney to Hobart yacht race.

A **fish shop** (above) in Sullivans Cove, Hobart

Apiarist Headley Hoskinson (right) tends his **bees** in Tassie's southern forests.

Harvesting the **hops** (below) at Ringwood's Bushy Park farm.

ISLAND ESCAPES

Tasmania's rich historical heritage and pristine environment make it an enchanting place to visit. Combine those with a wealth of gastronomic delights and fantastic walking and outdoor adventuring, and it's no wonder the Tasmanian tourist economy is booming. Gorgeous hotels, spas and rural retreats have sprung up all over the island, catering to a wide variety of tastes.

The Henry Jones Art Hotel in Hobart, for example, has won numerous travel awards, including gongs from Condé Nast and The National Architectural Awards. The hotel is housed in a row of old warehouses and a jam factory, and showcases Tasmanian art as well as having very plush rooms. Named after a former jam factory worker turned entrepreneur, the hotel draws inspiration from Tasmania's trade with the Far East, and each of its suites is named after a destination in Asia.

Far from the city, on the north-east corner of Tasmania and nestled in the Mount William National Park, is the Bay of Fires Lodge, an eco-lodge accessible only by foot. The surrounding area is a haven for wildlife, including eastern grey kangaroos, echidnas, brushtail possums, wombats, wallabies and Tasmanian devils.

Also off the beaten track is the unique Avalon Coastal Retreat. Built on a headland overlooking Great Oyster Bay and the Tasman Sea, its views of Maria Island to the south and Schouten Island to the north are fully exploited by its floor-to-ceiling windows. The attention to detail is wonderful: each room has an espresso machine, DVD player and heated polished concrete floors. No wonder it's so popular with honeymooners, who each get a free massage as part of their stay.

In the village of Evandale, you can travel back in time, at least for a long weekend, by staying at Strathmore, a convict-built residence completed in 1826 which now operates as a guesthouse. It is surrounded by extensive gardens, a large orchard and a lake perfect for gazing at while conjuring up pleasant daydreams.

Other travellers might search out something more active, such as the fly-fishing at Tarraleah in the Central Highlands. There you can stay at The Lodge, a five-star, Art Deco gem, which was, until recently, used by an entrepreneurial dominatrix to host kinky weekend parties!

The Islington Hotel, five-star boutique accommodation in Hobart.

The minimalist timber and glass interiors of the **Bay of Fires Lodge** blend beautifully with the pristine environment of Mount William National Park.

Gorgeous hotels, spas and rural retreats have sprung up all over the island, catering to a wide variety of tastes.

SPORTFILE

I n early 2007, a very strange thing happened. A Tasmanian sporting team beat off its bigger, richer, more experienced mainland rivals to win a national sporting competition. Like David versus Goliath, the Tasmanian Tigers thrashed New South Wales by 421 runs to win the national cricket trophy, 25 years after Tassie earned full-time status in the interstate competition. Even Tasmanian and Australian cricketing icon David 'Boonie' Boon was emotional, saying, 'It's the proudest day I have experienced in cricket.'

Due to their smaller population and fewer potential sponsorship dollars, Tasmanians have to do without a team in many of the national sporting competitions. They don't have an AFL team, for example, or an NRL team, or an NBL or A-League soccer team. Mostly they play amongst themselves or pick a club to support from elsewhere; many barrack for Melbourne clubs.

Tasmanians realised long ago that there is more to life than chasing after an inflated piece of pigskin – or watching others do it. To put it simply, they're the outdoors types, taking advantage of Tasmania's stunning array of natural landscapes and wilderness to go white-water rafting on the Franklin River, skiing at Ben Lomond, climbing on a rock face or fly fishing in a river somewhere.

The truly hardcore outdoors types compete in the yearly Three Peaks Race, in which teams sail 335 nautical miles and run 131 kilometres, ascending a total of more than two kilometres' worth of mountains in a madcap test of endurance that could only have been based on the idea of a Brit.

Trout fishing on Somercotes estate near Ross in the Central Midlands.

Cyclists on the **Greay Tasmanian Bike Ride** (main picture) passing through Bridestowe Estate Lavender Farm.

John Williamson, in his 1960 Austin Healey Sprite, on day two of **Targa Tasmania** (below).

Rafting through Irenabyss (right).

Maybe the most British of sporting pursuits in Tassie, however, is the annual Targa Tasmania, a five-day tarmac rally that takes all comers, from vintage MGs to modern racing cars. It is the automotive enthusiast's favourite outing of the year, except perhaps for the bumpy crossing of the notoriously rough Bass Strait.

FIVE OF THE BEST ... LONG DISTANCE WALKS

Frenchmans Cap an arduous track to the summit of the white quartzite dome of Frenchmans Cap (1446 metres), the most prominent peak in the Franklin–Gordon Wild Rivers National Park. **23 km.**

Maria Island Mercury Passage, Chinaman's Bay, Shoal Bay, the convict cells at Point Lesueur, the ochre pit at Bloodstone Point, Mount Maria, the restored convict settlement of Darlington, an Australian fur seal colony and an historic home once occupied by Italian entrepreneur, Diego Bernacchi. Easy. **30 km.**

Freycinet Peninsula Circuit around the Hazard Mountains to Hazards Beach, south to Cooks and Bryans Beaches, across heathland next to Mount Freycinet then descending to the white, quartz sands of Wineglass Bay. **30 km.**

The Tasman Coastal Trail a three- to five-day trek along the clifftops from Waterfall Bay through to Fortescue Beach, out to Cape Hauy and on to Cape Pillar. **45 km.**

The Overland Track a true wilderness great from Cradle Mountain to Lake St Clair, passing dolerite mountains, stunning waterfalls, a variety of ecosystems and Tasmania's highest mountain, before finishing at Australia's deepest lake. **65 km.**

NATURALWONDERS

The South-West National Park is one of the most isolated and untouched parts of the world.

More than a third of the state is reserved in a network of national parks, reserves and the Tasmanian Wilderness World Heritage Area, a refuge for rare plants and animals, including survivors of the ancient super-continent, Gondwana. As such, it's also a haven for lovers of nature, from birdwatchers and eco-tourists to bushwalkers and scuba divers.

The state's best known wilderness area is perhaps the superb Cradle Mountain–Lake St Clair National Park. The mountain, named by the surveyor Joseph Fossey in 1827 for its distinctive shape, is surrounded by native deciduous beech trees, rainforest, alpine heathlands, buttongrass and wide open moorlands. The walk to the peak, 1545 metres above sea level, is an eight-hour round trip. The park is one of the most glaciated areas in Australia and also includes Mount Ossey, Tasmania's highest mountain at 1617 metres, as well as Lake St Clair, Australia's deepest natural freshwater lake.

Further south is the Franklin–Gordon Wild Rivers National Park, where the Franklin and Olga rivers roar through rainforest shrouded in mountains. Much of the park is impenetrable rainforest, but the bushwalking is excellent in regions like Frenchmans Cap. With its deep gorges and raging rapids, it is also a spectacular spot for white-water rafting.

The Franklin and Gordon rivers were the cause of controversy in the 1980s when the state government planned to dam them for hydro-electricity, but the scheme was quashed by a high-profile environmental campaign, which put Tasmania on the map for its pioneering Green movement.

Although the south and east of the island is relatively well populated, the west is rugged, remote and formidable, with treacherous coast, wild rainforest, ancient rivers and tranquil valleys all within a relatively small area. The South-West National Park is one of the most isolated and untouched parts of the world. It is home to some of the planet's last pieces of virgin temperate rainforest. Here the Huon Pine, much sought after by Tasmania's colonists, is endemic, as is the swamp gum, the world's tallest hardwood and flowering plant. About 300 species of lichen, moss and fern live in the forest, glacial tarns dot the landscape, and in summer the alpine meadows bloom with wildflowers. Lake Pedder, so big it holds 27 times the volume of water in Sydney Harbour, is considered the jewel of this incredible and ancient region.

There's no room to describe the other incredible natural landmarks of Tasmania, but they include among them the limestone caves of Mole Creek, the magnificent Cataract Gorge in Launceston, and the mighty pink granite ridges of the Hazards, at Freycinet National Park.

Autumn colours in the **Walls of Jerusalem** (above).

The stunning reflections of **Cradle Mountain in Lake Dove** (main picture).

Sea planes at **Franklin-Gordon Wild Rivers** National Park (below).

The magnificent sight of **Wineglass Bay** (above) as seen from the Hazards lookout, Freycinet.

Great Oyster Bay (left), off the east coast.

BEACHESANDCOAST

If asked to name the country's most spectacular beaches, the mind does not automatically leap to Tasmania. But that's only because, as with much of the Apple Isle, the treasures of its untouched coast are well hidden, which makes them all the more magical.

The north and east have many spectacular white-sand beaches, including the picturesque spots of Binalong Bay, Sloop Rock and Stieglitz. The east coast is also the 'sun coast' because of its agreeable climate, and is home to Wineglass Bay on the Freycinet Peninsula, a perfect curve of white sand and blue sea which was named one of the ten best beaches in the world by the editors of Frommer's travel guides.

Down on the Tasman Peninsula, you'll find steep cliffs and unusual rock formations that seem aptly placed at the end of the earth, such as the roaring waters of the Devil's Kitchen, the fierce Blowhole, and the almost-too-geometrical-for-nature Tessellated Pavement. Nearby is Remarkable Cave, which you can walk through when the tide is out.

The west coast is equally wild, which is bad news for swimmers but good news for surfers. Serious Tasmanian waxheads can't go past the break at Marrawah. This small town is the westernmost settlement in Tasmania, and is also the home of important Aboriginal carvings at Mt Cameron West and Sundown Point.

Tasmania doesn't consist of just one island, and its smaller satellites all have their attractions. King Island in the Bass Strait, for example, provides views to the mainland on a clear day. Although known for its pretty beaches and lagoons, the tumultuous seas around the island conceal more than 70 shipwrecks. Up in the north-east is Flinders Island, which has dramatic

granite cliffs, as well as good scuba diving and fishing. And down in the south-east, you can find Maria Island, the whole of which was declared a national park in 1972. It features magnificent limestone cliffs, sandy beaches, forests, fern gullies and sandstone packed with fossils.

A king crab, and the pure-white sands and crystal waters of **Boat Harbour Beach**.

Sydney schmydney. New South Wha? Ask a Victorian and they will tell you that the Garden State is the economic capital, the sporting capital, the cultural capital, the comedy capital, the botanical capital, and the food and wine capital of Australia. Oh, and it should have been the political capital, too. They might even be right.

VICTORIA

The bustling laneway of **Block Place**, off Little Collins Street in Melbourne's CBD.

STATEFILE

Victorians are proud of their state, and rightly so, but they have always been touchy about comparisons with their larger neighbour to the north, so they might not like to be reminded that the state's first settlement was founded with Sydney's discards.

In 1803 the HMS *Calcutta*, loaded with convicts and a few free men, was diverted to Port Phillip, in modern-day Victoria, to ease the pressure on food resources at the Port Jackson colony. But the ship's captain quickly decided the spot was unsuitable for settlement and the whole party was moved to the fledgling colony at Hobart.

For the next 20 years the south-east corner of Australia was sparsely populated, except for a few sealers and whalers on the coast. However, in 1834 a group of eight entrepreneurs from Launceston in Van Diemen's Land (Tasmania) were looking for good pastoral land and decided to begin a European settlement on the north coast of the Bass Strait. When an expedition from Sydney arrived in the region a year later, they were surprised to find a small but thriving community there already.

Melbourne was founded in the same year by another Tasmanian, John Batman, and the town grew quickly. The state's first hankerings for independence came soon after, in 1840, when the Commissioner for Crown Lands in the Port Phillip district, Henry Fyshe Gisborne, presented the governor with a petition for separation from New South Wales. The petition was rejected, but in 1851 Queen Victoria signed the British Act of Parliament separating Victoria from New South Wales. The new colony was named in her honour and gained itself a constitution.

Some of the first motorists on the **Great Ocean Road** in 1932. It was built by returned serviceman mostly by hand.

VITAL STATISTICS

NICKNAME:	the Garden State
AREA:	237,629 km² (6th)
POPULATION:	5,110,500 (2nd)
POPULATION DENSITY:	22.47 people per km² (2nd)
LANDMARKS:	Bells Beach, Federation Square, Flinders Street Station, the MCG, the Twelve Apostles, Yarra Valley
INDUSTRIES:	finance, insurance and property services, community, social services, manufacturing, agriculture
SPORTS:	AFL, horse racing, tennis, golf, cricket
NATIONAL PARKS:	38, including Dandenong Ranges, Mornington Peninsula, Snowy River, Grampians, Wilsons Promontory
WORLD HERITAGE SITES:	Royal Exhibition Building and Carlton Gardens

The **Royal Arcade, Melbourne**, painted by ST Gill around 1854.

DID YOU KNOW?

When the HMS *Calcutta* abandoned Port Phillip in 1803, one convict managed to escape. William Buckley was given up for dead, but actually made contact with a number of Aboriginal families, settled, married and lived happily among the Watourong tribe on the Bellarine Peninsula. He didn't encounter another white man until 1835, and is thought to have inspired the phrase '**Buckley's chance**'.

In the same year as independence, gold was discovered near Ballarat, followed by strikes at Bendigo and across Victoria. It was the start of one of the biggest gold rushes ever – in ten years the population of the colony increased sevenfold, from 76,000 to 540,000. Immigrants arrived from all over the world, particularly China and Ireland, to take advantage of the new-found treasure. In the decade from 1851, Victoria produced 20 million ounces of gold, one-third of the world's output at the time.

In 1854 in Ballarat there was an armed rebellion against the British government troops, by disgruntled miners who felt the mining taxes being levied were unjust. Some of the leaders of the Eureka Stockade, as it became known, later became members of Victoria's parliament and the rebellion is still seen as a key moment in Australia's history.

In 1901 Victoria became part of the Federation of the Commonwealth, and because of its prosperity from the gold rush, was established as the financial capital of Australia. It was also the political capital between 1901 and 1927, while Canberra was being built.

Post-World War II immigration changed the face of the state; immigrants from Greece, Italy and Germany transformed the suburbs of Melbourne and brought with them the foods and languages of their homelands.

During the early 1990s Victoria experienced an economic slump, hastened by the collapse of the State Bank. Unemployment grew and many moved interstate, but this trend was reversed in the mid-1990s when the government began an aggressive program of public works around Melbourne to boost economic activity.

VICTORIATODAY

Victoria is the second largest state in terms of population and gross state product, but in terms of culture, she is no one's bridesmaid. Melbourne, with its wealth of theatre, dance, live music and vibrant restaurants, combined with its almost religious interest in sport, is widely considered the artistic and sporting capital of Australia.

Victoria is also a leader in education. The University of Melbourne enrolled its first student in 1855 and was the first in Australia to offer degrees. Today the state has nine universities, and Monash University, with nearly 56,000 students, is the largest in Australia.

The Victorian economy accounts for a quarter of the gross domestic product, and is largely reliant on its financial, insurance and property services, followed by the social services sector and manufacturing. With around 60 per cent of the state's land dedicated to farming, Victoria also manages to contribute around a quarter of the country's total agricultural value. Not bad, considering it is the smallest in land area of all the mainland states, and was not properly settled until the mid-19th century.

After Tasmania, Melbourne is known for its 'four seasons in one day' weather patterns; its cool winter temperatures and grey skies lead to many jibes from the more northern states. But many Victorians like it that way, and the climate is actually quite varied – from semi-arid and hot in the north-west to cool on the coast.

Cattle graze by the vineyards in the misty **Yarra Valley**.

SIGNS OF GOVERNMENT

Victoria's **coat of arms** features a blue shield bearing the Southern Cross. A kangaroo stands above holding a crown, signifying the British crown. On either side is a female figure representing Peace and Prosperity, which is also the motto displayed beneath the shield.

Victoria was the first Australian colony to have its own **flag**; it was first flown in 1870. It features the Union Jack, the Southern Cross and the Imperial Crown.

Parliament House, with its sweeping steps, grand colonnade and elegant lamps, is the largest public building in Australia. But it is incomplete according to the original plans; it was meant to be topped with a dome.

NATURAL AMBASSADORS

The **pink common heath** grows naturally in Victoria's coastal heathlands and subalpine country.

The endangered **Leadbeater's possum** lives only in Victoria. Its social structure, in which females are dominant, is unique among mammals – well, almost unique.

The brilliantly coloured **helmeted honeyeater** is under threat of extinction and is now found in only a small area around Woori Yallock Creek on the outskirts of Melbourne.

The timid **weedy seadragon** is Victoria's marine emblem and is found only in southern waters.

PEOPLEFILE

Since Federation in 1901, the Victorian population has more than quadrupled, from 1.2 million to more than five million today. The first European Victorians were Anglo-Celtic, but successive waves of immigrants from southern and eastern Europe, South-East Asia, the Middle East and Africa have added greatly to the ethnic mix and cultural life of the state.

Fruit sellers at **Queen Victoria Market**.

Members of the **Country Fire Authority** fight a bushfire on the Mornington Peninsula. The organisation has around 58,000 volunteers.

MOST LIKELY TO SAY:

Don't forget your umbrella and sunscreen.
Did you know this is the world's most liveable city?
A double decaf, skim soy latte, please.

LEAST LIKELY TO SAY:

I'd rather live in Sydney.
I much prefer rugby to AFL, anyway.
I don't do foreign-language films.

The **MCG crowd** performs a banned Mexican wave at the One Day Cricket International.

Nonetheless, the Victorian population is ageing rapidly and the state government predicts nearly 25 per cent will be over 60 by 2021. This has led to a population drive called 'Beyond Five Million', to encourage migration, regional population and family formation. The population of regional Victoria is growing healthily – in 2005 it grew by 1.3 per cent, to over 1.3 million.

However, the state as a whole is very urbanised. More than 90 per cent of Victorians live in towns and cities. The metropolitan area of Melbourne is home to about 3.7 million, with other major centres including Geelong, Ballarat, Bendigo and Mildura.

Just over 70 per cent of Victorians are Australian-born, but this figure falls to about 65 per cent in Melbourne, which is a proud multicultural melting pot with a particularly large Greek population. Almost 30 per cent of Melburnians speak a language other than English at home, and, in the state as a whole, a total of 180 languages are spoken.

LOCALLEGENDS

Ned Kelly throughout his youth Ned Kelly served time for various assaults and thefts, but in 1878 he was accused of assaulting a policeman, Constable Alexander Fitzpatrick, and went into hiding with his brother Dan and friends Joe Byrne and Steve Hart. They were pursued by police, but Ned's gang ambushed the police at Stringybark Creek, killing three. The Kelly Gang went on to rob the banks of Euroa and Jerilderie; at the latter, they had the nerve to dress as police. Ned also tried, in vain, to publish his Jerilderie Letter, which railed against the treatment of his family by the authorities and, more generally, the persecution of Irish Catholics.

In June 1880 the gang holed themselves up at the Glenrowan Inn. Here they made and donned their famous armour, as they waited for police. Ned was the only gang member to survive the ensuing ambush, and was tried and sentenced to death later that year. Despite a petition of about 32,000 signatures, he was hanged on 11 November 1880 at Melbourne Jail. He soon became an integral part of Australian folklore, mythologised as the larrikin lawbreaker who stood up to unjust authority.

Victoria may be Australia's smallest state, but it punches well above its weight when it comes to producing fascinating people, successful in all sorts of endeavours from politics to painting.

Alfred Deakin, Australia's second prime minister and one of the 'fathers of Federation', was a Victorian. Despite a long and interesting career in politics, he was also a prolific journalist and was universally liked – his nickname was 'Affable Alfred'.

Sir Isaac Isaacs was another Melbourne-born politician, who began life as the son of a Jewish tailor and went on to become the country's first Australian-born Governor-General in 1930. Sir Robert Menzies, Australia's longest-serving prime minister, was also a Victorian.

Controversial historian Geoffrey Blainey is also a Melbourne man, who began his academic career at Melbourne University. On the other side of the political spectrum is another Melbourne University alumnus, Germaine Greer. Greer grew up in the suburb of Mentone, and eventually went on to produce the groundbreaking feminist book *The Female Eunuch*.

Victoria has also produced some of Australia's best artists, writers and performers, including writers Helen Garner and Kate Constable; artists Frederick McCubbin and Arthur Streeton; actors Geoffrey Rush, Eric Bana and Guy Pearce; singers Kylie Minogue, Nick Cave and John Farnham; and, of course, Barry Humphries, whose alter-egos include Dame Edna Everage, a Melbourne housewife, and Sir Les Patterson, the foul-mouthed cultural attaché to Britain.

Dame Edna Everage
(aka Barry Humphries) –
a typical Melbourne
housewife.

CITYSTYLE

As the building work neared completion on Melbourne's unorthodox Federation Square development in 2002, Australia's second-largest city was divided over the results that were taking shape. Now, however, it has been become a popular addition to Melbourne's rich and varied cityscape.

In the run-up to its completion, Fed Square appeared to be a pile of copper, zinc, glass and asymmetrical boulders of Kimberley sandstone at an intersection that was always 100 per cent Melbourne, near the regal Flinders Street Station, the neo-Gothic St Paul's Cathedral, Melbourne's oldest pub Young & Jackson's, and just across the muddy Yarra, the piped caps, knitted vests and boat shoes of the city's private school rowing sheds. Would it work?

YOU KNOW YOU'RE A LOCAL WHEN ...

... you understand the **hook turn**. In Melbourne, thanks to the ubiquitous tram network, when you want to turn right across a tram track, you must pull into the left lane, wait for the lights to turn amber, and then execute. Also, drivers can only overtake trams on the left and must stop when a tram stops to let off passengers, if there is no central pedestrian island. The other catch is that the hook turn rule only applies in the city, virtually ensuring that visiting drivers will be exposed as foreigners, sooner or later, at which point locals take great pleasure in giving them a playful blast of the horn.

Federation Square (main picture) opened in 2002 on the former site of the unpopular 'Gas and Fuel' towers. With its cafés and cultural centres, it has become a popular public destination.

The **Royal Exhibition Building** (left) in Carlton Gardens, opened in 1880, is World Heritage listed as one of the oldest of its kind.

'Everyone's talking about it,' a nearby café owner, Mary, told *State of the Arts* magazine at the time.

'I don't think it blends in,' said a customer.

Several years on, Fed Square is the new heart of public Melbourne, its number one meeting point, arts destination and five o'clock beer spot. Its popularity is a testament to the city's love for getting together, its openness to new ideas even when surrounded by beautiful old ones, and its dedication to art and design as an integral part of everyday life.

Founded by entrepreneurs, built by convicts and bankrolled by gold money from nearby Bendigo and Ballarat, Melbourne is the traditional home of money and culture in Australia, even if Perth, Sydney and Adelaide rival it from time to time.

That history is encapsulated in Collins Street, which combines classic Victorian business architecture such as the Old Treasury Building with modern skyscrapers such as the Rialto. The business hub at the western end segues into the so-called 'Paris end of Collins Street' at the eastern – a sort of Victorian Fifth Avenue of high-end boutiques. The Melbourne Club, established in 1839, is also here, which has long been regarded as the networking hub and unofficial power centre of the business Establishment – although with no female members, its influence must be somewhat limited.

When Melburnians outgrew the city's Victorian grid streetplan last century, they moved across the river, where the kilometre-long Southgate Arts and Leisure Precinct and the Crown Entertainment Complex – simply 'Southbank' and 'Crown' to the locals – now teem with shoppers, eaters, thrillseekers and spectators. The casino caters to high rollers, punters and a large Chinese gambling community, which is why even the registration plates on limousines and shuttle buses carry lucky numbers.

Rooftop sculptures on a building in funky **Acland Street**, St Kilda.

THEMARVELSOFMELBOURNE

In annual liveability indexes, 'Marvellous Melbourne' routinely gets a mention as one of the world's best cities to call home. In fact, *The Economist* has twice named it at number one, because it's rich in culture, well-planned, affordable, economically strong, has good health care and low crime rates, and, last but not least, has what some would say is a pretty good climate.

Those liveability surveys also tend to revive the ages-old rivalry with the city's northern nemesis, Sydney. It doesn't matter so much where Melbourne finishes on the ladder, as long as it's somewhere above the bigger and brasher New South Wales capital.

Gallons of ink have been spilled and litres of hot air exhaled in debates over which city is superior, and still their inhabitants have been forced to agree to disagree. As we all know, the 1908 battle to become the capital ended in a tie, with Canberra being built especially for the purpose. But the act of comparison, singling out the little differences barely noticeable to visitors but blatantly obvious to locals, continues as a fun game.

While Melbourne drinks beer from pots, Sydney prefers schooners. Melbourne rides trams, Sydney has ferries. Melbourne loves Aussie Rules, Sydney flits between rugby league and union.

Arty, café-strewn **Brunswick Street**, Fitzroy, reflects the city's soul.

Geographically, Sydney sprawled too fast for itself while Melbourne grew carefully and gracefully, from its neat grid in the centre to bohemian Fitzroy and Mediterranean Carlton in the north; to Asian-flavoured Richmond in the east; south to WASPish South Yarra and Toorak; and further south to glitzy Prahran and sunny, hip St Kilda by the sea.

If they were continents, Melbourne would be Europe and Sydney North America. If films, they might be *Casablanca* and *Breakfast at Tiffany's*. If TV shows, maybe *Friends* and *Baywatch*. Bands? The Beatles and the Stones, perhaps. US cities: New York and LA.

We could go on all day. The rivalry never dies. Each city constantly inspires the other to bigger and better things.

Wrought-iron lacework (right) on a building in Carlton Terrace displays the splendour of the gold rush days.

Slick Mirvac **apartments in Docklands** (main picture) show the city is still booming.

The luxurious **Mariana Hardwick salon**, Fitzroy, offers the ultimate bridal shopping experience.

Lucy Hinckfuss in the window of **Le Louvre** – a fashion institution since 1922 at the 'Paris end of Collins Street'.

TREASURE TROVES

Hermon & Hermon dress your home as stylishly as you dress yourself at this fabulous furniture palace in Richmond; their policy is to stock only 'ooh-aah' merchandise.

Cacao a feast of hand-made chocolates and cakes in St Kilda.

Zetta Florence stacks of pretty paper, hand-bound journals and arty cards in Brunswick Street, Fitzroy.

Christine bow down to the goddess of accessories at this unique boutique in Flinders Lane.

Market Import browse through furniture, lamps and glassware from around the world at this kaleidoscope of colour in Armadale.

Philippa's the critics agree, this is *the* place to go for rustic breads, cookies, cakes, savouries and all such tempting treats.

RETAILTHERAPY

To the fashion-conscious, Melbourne is not about food, theatre or bars. It is about shopping – designer shopping, accessories shopping, chocolate, crafts and clothes shopping.

The CBD is home to all the usual international labels, including Versace, Max Mara and Cartier, but the more quirky spending opportunities are found in the Block and Royal Arcades – sumptuous examples of Victorian architecture and home to designer boutiques, cute cafés and specialty shops such as Haigh's Chocolate Shop and Block Arcade Coins. The Cathedral Arcade houses the Japanese-inspired delights of Genki, the unique and cool Alice Euphemia and the hip Route 66. On Presgrove Place is Smitten Kitten, which stocks flirty lingerie.

Flinders Lane is also a favourite. Here shoppers can browse various designer clothing stores as well as cute shops such as Christine, an accessories boutique, and Craft Victoria, which sells a distinctive array of pottery, jewellery, glassware and scarves.

Serious fashionistas head to Chapel Street for a fix – it has boutiques to die for, including Comme Il Faut, which showcases emerging new designers and one-off Australian designer accessories, and Nina Baird, a designer outlet store stocking European brands such as Gucci, Prada, Miu Miu and Fendi.

Chapel Street Bazaar, Prahan, offers an eclectic collection of bric-a-brac.

Melbourne is known for its vintage clothing scene. One of the best places to rummage is Retrostar Vintage in Cathedral Arcade. Its stock comes mainly from the United States and Canada, and includes airline totes, loud Pucci-style prints and shearling jackets straight from the '70s. The Shag stores, in three locations across the city, feature anything and everything from the 1980s back. Shag specialises in accessories, such as pre-loved compacts and Guerlain perfume bottles, and has a small collection of new clothing in the vintage vibe. Also stocking their own label next to vintage are the Hunter Gatherer stores in Fitzroy and St Kilda, which started as a student project but have since blossomed into successful businesses.

Alannah Hill
Autonomy
Bettina Liano
Jacqui Alexander
Jane Hill
J'Aton
Jenny Bannister
Jenny Hoo
Roy Christou
Saba
Scanlan & Theodore
Theresa Liano
Vicious Threads
Vixen
White Suede

FASHIONCAPITAL

A silver gown by Alex Perry at the launch of **L'Oreal Melbourne Fashion Week** 2007 in Government House.

The day after the annual Brownlow Medal Dinner, when the biggest prizes in AFL are handed out, newspapers and TV stations publish the results: glossy pictures of footballers' WAGs (Wives and Girlfriends) in jaw-dropping frocks. The players are routinely overshadowed by the clothes – or lack of them – paraded down the red carpet by their glamorous dates.

Recognition is almost as hard to come by for the thoroughbreds at the Spring Racing Carnival. The Makybe Divas and Doriemuses may be the stars of the show but the trackside divas attract more than their share of attention during the six weeks of horse races, 'fashion in the field' parades and champagne and canapés.

Melbourne is a stylish city. It loves to dress up and play with styles, cuts and fabrics. That's why others look to the Victorian capital's big events and signature labels for fashion tips.

Saba, founded in Melbourne in 1965, has become an enduring fixture of the Oz fashion scene, pioneering a contemporary take on women's and men's clothing.

The irrepressible Alannah Hill, although born in Tassie, brought fun back to fashion and reinvented boutique styling by dressing her sales assistants from head to toe like playful, blossoming flowers.

Scanlan & Theodore began on Chapel Street in the late 1980s, marrying conservative colours and fabrics with cutting edge designs in a style that many now consider 'very Melbourne'.

The annual L'Oreal Melbourne Fashion Festival in March has been showcasing the legends and the next breed of Melbourne fashion gurus for more than a decade. It differs from its Sydney sister-event because it sells tickets to the public and winds up with the always-quirky but usually entertaining Independent Runway show, featuring 15 new designers and their wackiest ideas, from remote control cars darting between the leggy models to men walking the runway in werewolf outfits.

MELTINGPOTCUISINE

It is often said that Melbourne has more Greeks than any other city in the world apart from Athens. It's not true, of course. For one thing, they are Greek-Australians now that they call Melbourne home. And secondly, the correct statistic is probably more like the third highest number of people of Greek heritage.

In any case, it is an illustration of how multicultural Melbourne is, which, as New York, London and Sydney will attest, always makes for good eating. Almost 30 per cent of Melburnians speak a language other than English at home, according to census data – the top five being Italian, Greek, Vietnamese, Cantonese and Arabic.

You can see the clusters of these cultures and others in Melbourne's eat streets. Little Bourke Street is the centre of Chinatown, marked by gates at each end but now expanded beyond its boundaries.

Lygon Street in Carlton is the city's Little Italy, where diners litter the wide footpaths outside trattoria after pizzeria after ristorante. Local folklore says – again, a difficult one to prove – that nowhere outside Rome will you find a greater concentration of pasta restaurants.

Not far to the east, trendy Brunswick Street is lined with cool cafés, bars and restaurants full of eccentric students and hipsters. Polly, for example, is like a timewarp for

White walls and wine at **Verge** restaurant.

drinkers who prefer their martini not shaken, not stirred, but served in the 1920s, please.

In Swan Street, Richmond, the Vietnamese community dishes up steaming pho and noodles, while the Jewish community can take most of the credit for St Kilda's spectacular cake shops.

Drawing on these diverse influences, Melbourne's best chefs have created unique concept restaurants and made Melbourne a world-class place to stuff your face. In the city the fine diners get their fix at Vue de monde, MoVida, Yu-U, ezard, Taxi and Flower Drum. In Windsor, diners eat only entree-sized dishes – because you can fit more in that way – at Jacques Reymond's converted Victorian mansion. In Fitzroy, it's the Enoteca and Ladro. In St Kilda, it's Circa the Prince or the Melbourne Wine Room. In Richmond, Pearl.

Then there are the restaurateurs for whom hats are simply something to keep the sun off. In 2007 Shanaka Fernando won the Australia Day Local Hero award for Lentil as Anything, an organic, vegan restaurant off Acland Street with a great name and a greater concept – you pay whatever you think the meal was worth. Fernando calls it 'a social experiment that encourages people to have an internal conversation with their conscience and their own ethics'.

HIDE AND DRINK

As coffee-addicted as Melbourne is, the city's obsession with liquid refreshment doesn't begin and end with the perfect cup of java. In the 1996 movie *Swingers*, Jon Favreau's character says that LA bars are hidden away in back alleys as a test of drinkers' knowledge. Melbourne is much the same. Its network of alleyways and its deregulated liquor licensing laws have given bar hoppers in the Victorian capital a smorgasbord of small, quirky, sometimes-very-well-hidden watering holes to dip in and out of. Take the Croft Institute, for example, which is styled like a high school science laboratory and gymnasium and tucked around three bends in Croft Lane. Or there's Misty, which eschews a sign out the front. Or St Jeromes in Caledonian Lane, the very little bar, barely 8 x 5 metres, that's a café by day, but a temple of funky electronica by night. It even gave rise to its own interstate music festival. Remember, though, if you have to ask where a bar is, you're clearly not cool enough to be there.

A NODE TO FINE DINING

It was a fizzer, a popped balloon, an anticlimactic end to the Melbourne food and wine world's night of nights.

Every second year, Melbourne's restaurateurs, critics and chefs gather to eat, drink, gossip and learn who has taken out the coveted industry awards in the city's foodie Bible, *The Age Good Food Guide*. A win can make a restaurant, while a drop from two hats to one – or none – can break it.

But in 2005, what happened was something quite different altogether. One of the most coveted gongs, Best New Restaurant, was 'not awarded'. Vue de monde, the mid-city French restaurant of culinary wonderboy Shannon Bennett, had looked set for the trophy after moving from Carlton to new digs in the CBD, but was deemed not 'new' enough by the judges.

Two years later, however, Bennett and Vue de monde more than made up for it when they scored three hats and an almost-perfect score in the 2007 *Good Food Guide* Awards.

'I think this is the first time the guide has given a 19 out of 20,' said Necia Wilden, its co-editor. 'Vue de monde is such a tremendously exciting restaurant … It dared to defy this trend away from fine dining. It's the glorious exception that proves the rule.'

The degustation at Vue de monde starts at about $150 for five or six

courses and rises to almost double that for the Gastronome's Menu, made up of dishes that Bennett thinks are the best and freshest that particular day.

The ingredients and the setting are not overly casual. The menu is packed with delicacies such as rich foie gras and black truffles, and the tables are set with hand-forged Laguiole cutlery. But the recipes are open-minded and at times sacrilegious.

Bennett, a shaggy-haired celebrity chef in the Jamie Oliver mould, first grabbed attention for his modern interpretations of classic creations, such as a $140 Wagyu beef burger served with a glass of Penfold's Grange. These days he makes headlines for extravagances such as hosting a ten-course degustation meal during the Melbourne Food and Wine Festival, inspired by ten different vintages of Chateau Petrus. On the menu:

Vue de monde's exquisite **interior** at Normanby Chambers.

a classic truffle risotto, beetroot-cured whiting with asparagus froth, twelve-hour roasted pork, hay-flavoured lamb galette and wild hare. The bill: a snip at $10,000 a head.

At press time, there was even some suggestion that Bennett might have won the ultimate honour in Melbourne society circles – a cameo on the hit comedy series *Kath & Kim*.

Escargot dans le jardin snail and chicken mousse set back into the shell, with parsley purée and parsley paper

Bouillabaisse 5 minute bouillabaisse, tartare of crayfish and buffalo milk skin, finished with aromatic herbs and caviar

Risotto au choux fleur cauliflower risotto with tarragon sabayon and parmesan ice
Or
Risotto aux cèpes ferron arborio risotto infused with cèpes

Terrine de lapin avec une mousse de foie gras terrine of rabbit with foie gras and pistachio mousse

Morue de Murray Murray cod, seven years old, cooked 'en sous-vide' with a ginger and spring onion sauce, flavoured with spring onion and crispy chicken skin

Consommé froid à la tomate delicate tomato consommé with gazpacho jelly

Salade de cochonaille salad of Kurobuta pork and black pudding with cider-marinated carrot ribbons, finished with emulsified pan juices.

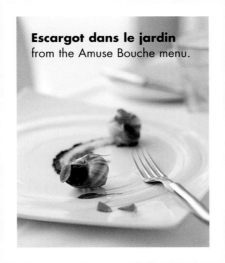

Escargot dans le jardin
from the Amuse Bouche menu.

'It dared to defy this trend away from fine dining.'

Fondue de boeuf wagyu grade 12 Wagyu served into a beef consommé topped with a beer air, partnered with fried shallots, pomme mille feuille, spinach mousse and a beignet of bone marrow
Or
Pigeon au chocolat pigeon cooked in chocolate with crispy leg meat, raw radish and sweet corn finished with chocolate oil

Fromage Roy de Vallées with marinated beetroot Pyrénées

Lollipop

Tarte aux pommes reconstructed apple tart

'Cheesecake' aux fruits de la passion passionfruit cream with frangipane sand and passion-fruit soufflé

Cigare au chocolat Valhrona chocolate roll filled with smoked chocolate and rolled in puff pastry 'cigar' leaves

Notre sélection de cafés, thés, infusions et petits-fours a selection of coffee, teas, infusions and miniature teacakes

Chocolates to take home

THE GARDEN STATE

The New Zealand-fronted, Melbourne-formed band Crowded House famously wrote about Melbourne's climate in the song 'Four Seasons in One Day', borrowing a phrase often used to describe the unpredictable weather at the top of Port Phillip Bay.

Sydneysiders have been known to be somewhat more cruel about Melbourne's grey skies and call it the 'Bleak City', but the plants don't seem to mind the mild weather at all. From its very beginning, this has been a city with a big green thumb, leading to Victoria's nickname of 'The Garden State'.

In 1851, when it was announced that they would be free of New South Wales to form their own colony, the first Victorians celebrated under what is now called 'the Separation Tree', a red gum in the Royal Botanic Gardens. Nearby is La Trobe Cottage, once the home of Charles La Trobe, the first Governor of Victoria. So Victoria's roots, appropriately, now lie protected in its premier park.

Also in the Botanic Gardens are 36 hectares of lush green space plus plant specimens gathered by the botanist Joseph Banks who travelled to Australia with Captain Cook on the *Endeavour*. Cook's parents lived in a little cottage in Yorskhire, England. That is, it was in Yorkshire, England until it was dismantled, packed up and shipped to Fitzroy Gardens east of Melbourne's CBD.

In total there are nearly 480 hectares of parks and gardens in Melbourne. As the Fitzroy and Botanic Gardens hem the city in on one side, along with Birrarung Marr and Kings Domain, the Carlton Gardens are its lungs on the other. All are popular places to escape to on weekends or at lunchtimes.

The Victorian obsession with flora is not merely a public one – it extends into people's backyards too. This was where Australia's Open Garden Scheme started in 1987. Today, it has more than 5000 of the country's 'most inspiring private gardens' on its books, periodically opening them for public viewing.

However, there is one thing that has changed little since Melbourne was founded:

The whimsical gates of a nursery in **Brunswick Street**, Fitzroy.

St Kilda pier (main picture) at sunset.

Fitzroy Gardens (below) on a misty autumn morning.

DID YOU KNOW?

On Port Phillip Bay, St Kilda faces the city's other romantic expanse of water. **Paul Kelly** rhapsodises about it in his song 'From St Kilda to Kings Cross', when he sings 'I'd give you all of Sydney Harbour (all that land, all that water) for that one sweet promenade.' Kelly's evocative and parochial lyrics have become part of the state's high school English syllabus.

the Yarra River that divides the city in two. While the old joke is that the Yarra 'flows upside down', because the water is somewhat brown in hue, it is actually a habitat for many fish and one of the city's favourite settings for a romantic walk. Lovers can often be seen crossing the bridge at Flinders Street Station, turning left and strolling along the banks of the river past canoeists and rowers and through Alexandra Gardens to the Royal Botanic Gardens, perhaps stopping off for a picnic or a clinch on the grass.

BEACHLIVING

Victoria doesn't boast the postcard-worthy white sand beaches of Queensland, nor does it have a glamorous equivalent to New South Wales's Bondi Beach, but its coastline, little developed, peaceful and picturesque, has a relaxed lifestyle and a quirky charm that is completely its own.

The Bellarine Peninsula, on the west of Port Phillip Bay, has a string of beautiful beaches so popular with Melbourne's fashionable folk that real estate agents complain of severe shortages in holiday rentals. The beach at Queenscliff was an elegant seaside resort during the 19th century and has enjoyed a renaissance in recent years. Its gorgeous Victorian buildings have been renovated and turned into guest houses and restaurants for chi chi Victorians.

SEASCAPES: BATHING BOXES

The iconic bathing boxes of the **Mornington Peninsula** hark back to genteel Victorian times, when bathers needed discretion and privacy at the beach. There are about 1300 dotted along the peninsula, with a colourful concentration at Brighton Beach. Once considered little more than a local curiosity, these quirky little sheds are now valuable architecture and many are listed on the Victorian Heritage Register. Some are privately owned and others are licensed out by the local council. Licensees are allowed to make minor alterations, such as cornices or small mural designs — many of which are works of art in themselves.

Colourfully painted
bathing boxes
at Brighton Beach.

More low-key are the family-oriented St Leonards and Portarlington Beaches. Parts of the popular ABC television series *SeaChange* were filmed at St Leonards, but the majority of the show's action took place at Barwon Heads, which was a sleepy seaside town before the series put it on the tourist trail. Today more people than ever enjoy its rolling coastal dunes and stunning ocean views.

Further along the coast, on the Great Ocean Road – a drive so famous it has almost become a rite of passage for Australians and tourists alike – are the resorts of Lorne and Apollo Bay. Fashionable Lorne sits on the estuary of the Erskine River, with a backdrop of the emerald slopes of the Otway Ranges. Its fine old buildings and leisurely air keep the hordes coming back every summer. It's a renowned fishing spot, as is Apollo Bay, a more relaxed and eclectic hangout further south, which is absurdly picturesque.

Great surfing can also be found along this stretch, notably at the unofficial surf capital of Australia, Torquay, and legendary Bells Beach, home to its own international surf competition and immortalised in the Hollywood movie *Point Break*.

On the other side of Port Phillip Bay is the equally popular Mornington Peninsula, the southernmost point of the Australian mainland, and home to an incredibly beautiful national park. Sorrento Beach, on the tip of the peninsula, is a charming and trendy resort with a lively main strip of restaurants, bars, cafés and ice cream parlours. The presence of traditional Aboriginal middens on the town's clifftops strongly suggest that modern-day Melburnians are not the first people to have loved this seaside spot.

Victoria also possesses lovely islands just off its coast – notably Phillip Island, which is popular with penguin watchers, who descend on the island every summer to watch tiny fairy penguins waddle up the beach to their nests at the end of a hard day's fishing. Isolated French Island, although only about 60 kilometres from Melbourne, is a blessed retreat for the environmentally minded (and for celebrities, notably 'our' Kylie, who has bought about 100 hectares of land). The tranquil island has been remained relatively undeveloped, with its small population using only alternative energy sources. It has recently been declared a state park.

Sand Sculpting Australia is a popular family event, the proceeds of which go to charity.

ATHOMEWITHNATURE

The iconic beach boxes of the Mornington Peninsula hark back to genteel Victorian times, but today's coastal architecture is just as distinctive. Style and the environment are often at their heart.

St Andrews Beach House on the Mornington Peninsula has been cited as one of the finest examples of contemporary Australian architecture. Designed by Sean Godsell Architects, the house is a box-like construction facing the southern ocean. It is protected from the elements by a galvanised steel outer skin, and made up of two discrete sections – a bedroom block and an open-plan living and kitchen block, connected by a deck, which residents have to traverse when walking between the two, exposing them to brutal wind in winter and harsh heat in summer.

This was done deliberately to provide an antidote to the sanitised, controlled environment of an office. The designers were influenced by other forms of Australian architecture, such as the Queenslander house, which welcome the seasons into the house.

In Warrnambool, at the western end of the Great Ocean Road, The Bird Residence is another architecturally designed home which takes full advantage of its spectacular ocean views. Conceived by Baldasso Cortese, the house is spacious and block-like, with internal courtyards and built-in screens creating privacy for family members.

The Coastal Residence at Dromana combines the typically Australian material of corrugated iron sheeting with luxury and space. The entire lower level is designed to be used only when children and grandchildren visit.

Frankston on Port Phillip Bay is home to the Architecture Treehouse Project, designed to save a 120-year-old Moreton Bay fig, which was being threatened by a developer. An architectural firm and the local council stepped in. They built units around the tree, with their foundations raised so as not to disturb the root system and to allow a sub-floor watering system to keep the soil damp. The

construction also has a top energy efficiency rating and was built using recycled materials, making it one of the worthiest of all Victoria's stylish seaside homes. The units were also sold for charity.

> An antidote to the sanitised, controlled environment of the office.

Houses line the idyllic shore of **Barwon Heads** (main picture) on the Bellarine Peninsula.

Architect Sean Godsell (left) and his award-winning beach house on the Mornington Peninsula.

COUNTRYSTYLE

The Botanical Gardens at **Ballarat**

Country Victoria is the land of hoteliers and rangers, vintners and shearers, where working farms plough the wealth of the land, while tired bodies are pampered in restored colonial buildings at some of the country's most luxurious modern resorts.

Paddle-steamers at Echuca on the Murray River.

The Wimmera region in the state's far west is spread with huge wheat fields and sheep farms, which form the backbone of Victoria's agricultural economy. Flour mills and grain silos dominate town skylines, while farming dominates conversations. Every Easter in Stawell, however, all minds turn to running; the town plays host to Australia's richest foot race, the Stawell Gift.

Further north, up on the Murray River, Mildura has a warm, dry Mediterranean climate, ideal for growing citrus fruit and vegetables. The town attracts hundreds of seasonal workers each year, as well as tourists, who come to take rides on the old paddle-steamers that ply the Murray. Thanks to Stefano de Pieri's *Gondola on the Murray* TV series and cookbooks, Mildura has also become a gourmand's mecca, and foodies flock to his award-winning restaurant to enjoy the ambience of its cellar setting, the area's fresh produce and Stefano's exquisite preparation techniques.

Swan Hill, also on the Murray River, earned its name when the early explorer Major Thomas Mitchell spent a night here in 1836 and was kept awake by noisy black swans. It has now grown into an attractive town with beautiful gardens and is known for its excellent fishing, particularly for its Murray cod.

The former gold towns of the state's centre are fascinating in their history, with Ballarat and Bendigo being the best known. Ballarat's rich diggings accounted for one quarter of all the gold mined in Victoria, and were only exhausted in 1918. Today the main street's glorious architecture and gorgeous gardens are a reminder of its riches. Bendigo has a remarkable ethnic history, owing to the thousands of Chinese immigrants who flocked here during the gold rush and who ended up staying. Its Joss House remains in use as a place of worship and is now protected by the National Trust.

With our growing interest in health in recent years, the twin towns of Daylesford and Hepburn Springs in the Central Highlands are enjoying a revival. Their mineral springs have earned them the name of the 'spa centre of Victoria'. Nearby Castlemaine is famous for liquid of a different kind – this is where Australia's XXXX beer was first brewed in 1859, before being moved to Brisbane.

FIVE OF THE BEST ... HEALTH SPAS

Mineral Spa Hepburn Springs established in 1895, this spa offers a wealth of luxurious treatments including Lomi Lomi, Thai and Hot Stone Massage, Shirodhara, Chinese Cupping, Vichy Shower, Scotch Hose and Clay Body Wraps.

Daylesford Day Spa located in a gorgeous heritage building, Daylesford prides itself on its earthy and harmonious ambience. Rose Milk Baths are counted amongst its treatments.

Shizuka Ryokan Day Spa Retreat this Japanese bath-house offers traditional treatments, from 'geisha' facials to a Yin and Yang package for couples.

Peppershell Place this spa specialises in massage and also provides packages for two, whether they're for couples, friends or mother-and-daughter outings.

Salus Spa at Lake House this spa's signature treatment is a tub filled with heated mineral water and aromatherapy oils, in a treetop cabin overlooking a lagoon.

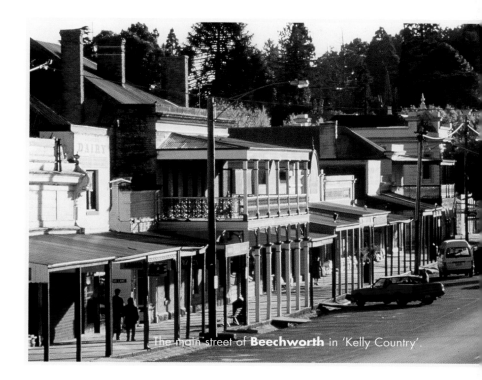

The main street of **Beechworth** in 'Kelly Country'.

Man's best friend, and swag, on the road in rural Victoria.

BUSHBOUNTY

With Melbourne as the unofficial foodies' capital of Australia, it's no surprise that the lush pastures and mountain ranges of Victoria support a wide variety of fresh produce, from milk and cheese through to wine and strawberries.

Central Gippsland is home to a strong dairy industry, which produces much of Melbourne's milk, as well as export cheeses, such as Gippsland Blue from the Tarago River Cheese company, and the award-winning Jindi Brie, made on a small farm at Jindivick.

These same pastures are also the grazing ground for stocks of beef and lamb, and during the warmer months, the orchards of the region are heaving with berries and fruit. Some, such as Drouin West Fruit and Berry Farm, open their doors to the public to pick what they like. And at the end of a hard afternoon's picking, you can sample some of the farm's boutique wines at its Berry Good Café. Delis in the region, notably Gippsland Food and Wine in Yarragon, sell locally grown produce including tomatoes, chestnuts and hazelnuts.

The Goulburn Valley on the NSW border is fertile farming land and makes a significant contribution to the state's agricultural wealth, particularly with fruit, vegetables, cereals and dairy products. It is also home to two fruit canneries, SPC and Ardmona.

Of course, Victoria also produces wine to wash down all that food. The state has 500 wineries, with cool varieties produced in the Macedon Ranges and warmer types coming from the Murray River region. But the best-known region is, without doubt, the Yarra Valley.

Although the Yarra Valley earned a good international reputation for its wine back in the 19th century, it wasn't until the late 20th century that the area gained its current status. Dr John Middleton, James Halliday, de Bortoli and Moet & Chandon all made their mark, and the region is now celebrated for its chardonnay, pinot noir and sparkling wines.

TASTE OF THE COUNTRY

Portarlington Mussels
Yarra Valley Pasta
Holy Goat Cheese
Milawa Cheese
Bress Cider
Sunny Ridge
Strawberries
Cheznuts Chestnuts
Mornington Peninsula Chocolates

As for world-class Victorian restaurants, Melbourne cannot claim a monopoly. Bendigo, for example, is home to Restaurant Bazzani, where diners can sit down to mouth-watering combinations such as ocean trout, goat's cheese and kaffir lime or roast rabbit with cauliflower cream. An historic building in nearby Ballarat is home to the Phoenix Brewery, where chef Simon Coghlan serves up magnificent dishes including slow-cooked duck ragout and tandoori Atlantic salmon with mash and field asparagus.

The Healesville Hotel and Chateau Yering in the Yarra Valley also have a strong reputation, as do the afternoon teas at the Rupertswood Mansion in Sunbury – birthplace of the Ashes – and fine dining at Campaspe Country House.

Victoria celebrates its fresh produce and wine with a host of festivals. There's the Shed Fest Wine Festival in October, accompanied by live music and old-fashioned games like petanque and croquet. The Mornington Peninsula hosts the Winter Indulgence Festival in June when local producers stage farmers' markets at winery cellar doors; and there's also the Strawberry Festival, which revolves around cream teas and a strawberry eating competition.

Alambie Wines
Best's
Brown Brothers
Dalwhinnie
Deakin Estate
Ghiran
Hanging Rock
Heathcote
Jenny Hoo
Mount Langhi
Pizzini
Seppelts Great
Tahbilk
Trentham Estate
Yarra Burn
Western

Yering Station winery (main picture), in the heart of the Yarra Valley, was Victoria's first vineyard, planted in 1838.

Apricots (left) ripe for picking at an orchard in Wandin.

SPORTFILE

I n the 1890s the American writer Mark Twain, creator of Tom Sawyer and Huckleberry Finn, observed this of Melbourne: 'It is the largest city of Australia, and fills the post with honour and credit. It has one speciality; this must not be jumbled in with those other things. It is the mitred Metropolitan of the Horse-Racing Cult.' Now, of course, you could substitute 'horse-racing' for 'sport' in general.

Melbourne is no longer the nation's biggest city, but it remains its horse-racing hub, with absolutely everything shutting down on the first Tuesday in November for the Melbourne Cup public holiday and effectively slowing down for the whole of the Spring Racing Carnival in October and November.

But other sports are followed here with equal religious fervour, and each of them has its own temple of worship. Indeed, when the Australian Empire declines and archaeologists pick over the ruins of Melbourne thousands of years from now, they will wonder why we needed so many big sporting venues.

The Melbourne Cricket Ground, home of cricket in Australia and venue of the AFL Grand Final, has been steadily extended since it opened in 1853 to the point where it now holds 100,000 people. The Melbourne Cricket Club has the biggest membership of any sporting club in Australia.

The nearby Telstra Dome – now the official home of the AFL administration – holds 53,400, while the Olympic Park Stadium – where the Melbourne Storm rugby league team plays – fits up to 18,500. Other venues are tiny in comparison. The nearby Rod Laver Arena, where the world's best tennis players fight it out for the Australian Open title in January, has a capacity of 15,000 people, and the Vodafone Arena, which hosts basketball, cycling and indoor tennis among other things, has seats for a mere 10,500 bums.

The Victorian government even gave Australian surfing a spiritual home in the 1970s, when it declared Bells Beach, near Torquay, the world's first surfing reserve. And to keep the global theme, since 1961 it has been attracting the world's best surfers for the world's longest running surfing competition, the Bells Beach Rip Curl Pro. In 2000 the beach and break were named a site of historical significance by the Victorian branch of the National Trust of Australia.

Melb

THE SPORTING CALENDAR

January the gold pyjamas are donned for cricket's One-Day International series finals, and faces are painted for the Australian Open.

February leave the flares at home, please, it's the A-League Grand Final (venue depends on qualifiers).

March the Formula One Grand Prix brings out the city's glamour set.

April surf's up for the Bells Beach Rip Curl Pro Surf Classic, then place your bets for The Stawell Gift professional sprint.

September the big one: the AFL Grand Final. Much to the dismay of clubs from other states, it is always played at the MCG.

October the suits, frocks and fascinators come out for the Spring Racing Carnival and the Melbourne Cup.

December Christmas recovery session begins at the Boxing Day Test Match.

Kelly Slater (main picture) in the **Rip Curl Pro** at iconic Bells Beach.

Roger Federer (left) in January 2007 winning the **Australian Open Tennis Championships**, held at the Rod Laver Arena.

Victorians will turn up in their tens of thousands to the competitive opening of a paper bag.

Opening of the **AFL Grand Final** (above top) at the MCG.

Young fans (above) get behind Collingwood and Melbourne.

Delta Blues (right) wins the **Melbourne Cup** in November 2006.

THESPECTATORSTATE

The latest evidence that Victorians will turn up in their tens of thousands to the competitive opening of a paper bag came when the Melbourne Victory soccer team was created in 2005 for the national A-League games. As one newspaper reported, the ancient ethnic divisions of the city's soccer fans were suddenly forgotten.

'Something remarkable is afoot in Melbourne,' the *Age* reported after game three. 'More than 11,000 turned up to Olympic Park on Monday night to watch Melbourne Victory's third win in a row … It was not just how many, but who. All the old factions were there – Greeks, Italians, Croats – but as one. They chanted for "Melbourne" and "Victoria".' Their support was rewarded; a year later, the Victory won the competition.

Victoria's reputation as the sporting capital of the nation is mostly proven by the statisticians' numbers. Of all the states in Australia, Victoria has the highest rate of attendance for the big sports and the ones that Victorians are known to love: horse racing, Australian Rules football, tennis, golf and cricket.

In terms of overall attendance at sporting events, 51.6 per cent of people in the Garden State attended sport once a year or more. Surprisingly, this puts it in second place behind South Australia, where it seems a higher attendance by women and a higher attendance at less popular sports pushed the Festival State into the number one position. Perhaps if watching sport were made into a sport itself, Victoria might raise its game.

WHAT IN THE WEIRD?

Country Victoria isn't all wine tasting and high tea. The Grand Prix at Edenhope is an event for speed freaks: and must be one of the world's only races for mobility scooters. Only legitimate drivers – the old or infirm – are allowed to compete, but it's a seriously contended race. Held on a street circuit, with grid girls, nasty chicanes and a tricky little roundabout at Apex Park, the race's competitors have been known to soup up their machines; having installed wider wheels, one pensioner, Theo Smoulders, was recorded reaching speeds of 19 km/h.

LIVINGLEGENDS

Whoever said that sport and politics don't mix clearly wasn't a Victorian. Down here, sporting heroes are so well-loved that they have a habit of rising to positions of power and influence when they retire.

Former Aussie Rules player Justin Madden became the state's sports minister after hanging up his footy boots in 1997 and then went on to organise the 2006 Commonwealth Games, while one-time aerial ski jumper Kirstie Marshall entered the Victorian upper house after coming back to earth in 1998. John Landy, who in 1954 became the second man ever to run a mile in under four minutes, was made Governor of Victoria.

Adulation for sports stars has been a way of life here since Phar Lap's golden days and his mysterious death in 1932. He has now become the Melbourne Museum's most popular exhibit, in all his stuffed glory.

These days, you need not even have been one of the players to ride the sporting escalator to success. Collingwood Football Club President Eddie McGuire ended up as host of the TV game show *Millionaire* and then (albeit briefly) CEO of Channel Nine, earning himself the nickname 'Eddie Everywhere'.

> Adulation for sports stars has been a way of life here since Phar Lap's glory days.

Shane Warne celebrates his 700th wicket at the Boxing Day Test, 2006

Craig Mottram training in the mountains of Falls Creek.

Craig Mottram, whose brother was in the gold-medal winning basketball team at the Commonwealth Games, has been challenging the all-conquering Africans at running over the 5000-metre distance, picking up a World Championships bronze in 2005. Could he be the next cultural attaché to Kenya?

There must be a role in Treasury for the maths genius and card sharp Joe Hachem, who was catapulted to stardom in 2005 after he won the World Series of Poker first prize of $7.5 million.

And what about NBA and Boomers basketball star Andrew Bogut, or Socceroos captain and Leeds United striker Mark Viduka? If those two can't help the state achieve its goals in the 21st century, who can?

And it works the other way in the Garden State, which could just as easily be called the Sporting State – the rich and powerful love to get involved in sport. Both John Elliott, one-time Liberal Party President and multi-millionaire, and Richard Pratt, one of Australia's richest men, have been president of the Carlton Football Club.

You have to wonder what it all means for the current crop of sporting legends. Shane Warne, the spin king of the MCG, retired from international cricket during the 2006/07 Ashes series while ranked as the greatest bowler ever. Will Victorians forgive 'Warnie' his marital indiscretions, flirtations with slimming drugs, cigarettes, bookmakers and other vices and appoint him the state's next Minister for Sport and Recreation, Gaming and Racing?

Nathan Buckley kicks out of centre in Collingwood v. Kangaroos.

ARTSANDCULTURE

When John Brack's painting *The Bar* sold for $3.1 million in 2006, it was an auction record for an Australian painting. It was also a painting of a Melbourne scene – the six o'clock swill in a 1950s pub – by a Melbourne artist, and was very nearly bought by the National Gallery of Victoria, which was knocked out of the bidding when it topped $3 million. Culture in Victoria makes money but, more importantly, it's a way of life.

The previous record for an Australian painting was held by *Bush Idyll*, a painting by another Melbourne artist, Frederick McCubbin, of the Victorian countryside. None of this is surprising to art aficionados, who know that most of Australia's collectors and valuable artworks live in Melbourne.

Brack's iconic *Collins Street, Melbourne, 5 O'Clock* hangs at the National Gallery of Victoria, whose Ian Potter Centre for Australian Art at Federation Square is prime real estate for an Australian painting. The NGV is Australia's oldest and most visited art gallery.

North at Carlton Gardens, the Melbourne Museum pioneered the new interactive model for museums that has been adopted at the National Museum in Canberra, while the Museum of Victoria has arguably the best collection of Aboriginal artefacts of any institution in the country.

Melbourne's theatres pull their weight too, from the magnificent Her Majesty's to the Regent, the Athenaeum, the Forum and the Palais. The Melbourne Theatre Company is Australia's oldest, and in recent years it has been our most successful at the annual Helpmann Awards for Aussie plays and musicals.

And where else in Australia would a new opera company spring up these days? As Australian opera and others lament the high cost of staging the most lavish artform humankind has invented and the loss of audiences to TV, video games and the internet, the Victorian government founded the Victorian Opera in 2006, with the attitude of 'hang the consequences'.

Two operas, two orchestras and the Australian Ballet now perform in Melbourne.

In a city where every empty space is a potential cinema or sculpture park and the walls around it are a blank canvas, what else would you expect?

The **Australian Ballet** production of *Don Quixote* at the State Theatre.

Rooftop cinema (main picture) in Swanston Street in Melbourne's CBD.

Street graffiti (below) in Brunswick Street.

READ ... WATCH ... LISTEN TO ...

True History of the Kelly Gang Peter Carey depicts country Victoria through the eyes of its most famous son.

The Getting of Wisdom set in a ladies' college in Melbourne, the book (by Henry Handel Richardson aka Ethel Richardson) was later made into a film.

Picnic at Hanging Rock Peter Weir's classic film (1975) tells the story of a disappearance, but put Australian films on the map.

Kenny the endearing 2006 mockumentary of the port-a-loo delivery guy has the tagline 'A knight in shining overalls'.

John Farnham the Voice has been an Aussie icon since 'Sadie (The Cleaning Lady)' reached number one back in 1967.

Nick Cave the boy from the country became a provocative player in the post-punk scene of the late '70s, before forming Nick Cave and the Bad Seeds, securing a dedicated worldwide following.

THEFESTIVALCALENDAR

JANUARY the Midsumma Festival kicks off the calendar with a knees-up to celebrate gay and lesbian culture in Victoria. Then Melbourne streets erupt with colour in the Chinese New Year celebrations, including Chinese opera, chess competitions, calligraphy, culinary delights and, of course, lion dances.

FEBRUARY a carnival atmosphere takes over the bayside suburb of St Kilda with music, costumes and a parade.

MARCH the Moomba Waterfest is one of the country's longest running festivals, with flying birdmen, water sport activities and celebrity challenges on the Yarra. Or enjoy the world's longest lunch at the Melbourne Food and Wine Festival – one of the best places a belly can be.

APRIL Victoria celebrates Anzac Day like the rest of the country: remembrance at dawn and then two-up 'til dusk. Some say it's more Australian than Australia Day. Then there's the unique Melbourne International Comedy Festival. Launched in 1987 by Barry Humphries and Peter Cook, the annual laughfest has become huge and is recognised as one of the world's top three comedy galas.

MAY Melbourne encourages young artists to express themselves in all media – text, sound, digital, visual – at the Next Wave Festival.

JULY watch flicks from more than 50 nations at the Melbourne International Film Festival.

AUGUST and then read books from around the world at the Melbourne Writers' Festival (or meet the people who wrote them).

SEPTEMBER indulge in olives and ouzo at the Antipodes Festival – the biggest celebration of Hellenic art and culture outside Greece. Then stock up on showbags at the Royal Melbourne Show. It started as a simple ploughing competition, but now the land has been coming to the big smoke for more than 150 years.

OCTOBER thousands of established acts and newer performers overwhelm you with choice at the Melbourne International Arts Festival and the Melbourne Fringe.

DECEMBER wrap up warmly and limber up your vocal chords for the Christmas tradition of Carols by Candlelight. The action happens at the Sidney Myer Music Bowl, named after Melbourne's department store founder and one of its biggest arts philanthropists.

WHAT IN THE WEIRD?

When director Richard Wolstencroft's 1999 film *Pearls Before Swine*, about an S&M- and Dr Who-loving hitman, missed out on selection for the Melbourne International Film Festival (MIFF), the director believed it was because his work was too confrontational and the main event had become too predictable. So Wolstencroft launched the Melbourne Underground Film Festival, or **MUFF**, and screened it himself. MUFF is an alternative program, featuring mostly adult, genre, contro-versial, avant garde, political, sexual or artistic concepts.

Carols by Candlelight (opposite) at the refurbished Sidney Myer Music Bowl.

Chinese New Year firecrackers (left) at the Quanh Minh Temple, Braybrook, Melbourne.

CURRENT DARLINGS

No one will ever be able to accuse Victorians of not being able to laugh at themselves. Some of their favourite characters and performers have gained notoriety by sending up themselves, their city and their state.

Dame Edna Everage may have pioneered the genre on stage, but this century the comedians Gina Riley and Jane Turner have taken it to a worldwide TV audience with their hugely successful *Kath & Kim* series, in which two 'foxy morons' from the mythical Fountain Lakes – a modern-day Moonee Ponds – deal with the ins and outs of modern life in what looks very much like the outer suburbs of Melbourne. All three – Edna Everage, Kath Day-Knight and Kim Craig – formed part of the entertainment at the 2006 Commonwealth Games.

Kath & Kim jumped from the ABC to the commercial network Channel Seven in 2007, as US producers began work on an American adaptation of the show. It has also been sold to the UK, Ireland and Finland.

In between the housewife gigastar and the mother-and-daughter hornbags, the Kerrigan family from *The Castle* (1997) had Australians everywhere rolling in the aisles as they attempted to save their runway-side home in Melbourne from the government and the airport corporation. Daryl Kerrigan (Michael Caton) took their case all the way to the High Court, where his inept lawyer (Tiriel

Kate Langbroek and **Ian 'Molly' Meldrum** (above) at the 2006 Logie Awards for *Dancing with the Stars*. Chris Cheney of **The Living End** (right) perform for Channel V at Federation Square.

Kylie's triumphant
return to the stage
in November 2006.

Kath and Kim provide
pre-match entertainment
at the MCG.

Mora) infamously argued that their eviction was contrary to 'the vibe' of the constitution.

The makers of that movie, who once formed most of the D-Generation comedy troupe and now run Working Dog productions, are a former Melbourne university clique who continue to make high-rating TV shows such as *The Panel* and *Thank God You're Here*.

One of *The Panel*'s panellists, Kate Langbroek, is a darling of FM radio thanks to her Nova 100 show with fellow Victorian comic Dave Hughes. Hughes was voted the favourite personality of Australian TV advertising audiences and therefore appears in several TV commercials for Holden and other companies.

Given the popularity and quality of the annual comedy festival, it's probably no coincidence that so many of the state's darlings are jokers. But that's not to say that the more 'serious' artists don't get their due. Kylie, although based in the UK, remains a favourite and a style role model, even though locals remember her perm in the *Neighbours* days. Singer-songwriter Paul Kelly is to Melbourne as Bob Dylan is to New York. The rock bands Jet and The Living End are proud local exports. Hollywood stars such as Radha Mitchell, Eric Bana and Hugh Jackman are widely adored.

Even an old rocker such as Ian 'Molly' Meldrum, who nurtured Australian popular music in its infancy as host of the ABC's *Countdown*, is still a local hero. He's the number one ticket holder at the St Kilda AFL club and the music guru for high-rating brekkie show *Sunrise*.

NATURALWONDERS

I n many ways Victoria is quiet and unassuming; small and tucked away in the corner of the continent, it is not as flashy as our other bigger and brassier tourist destinations, like Uluru or the Barrier Reef. And yet its natural wonders are as awe-inspiring and varied as they come, from rock formations to marine parks, from beaches to eucalypt forests.

The Twelve Apostles on Victoria's Great Ocean Road once went by the more prosaic moniker of 'Sow and Piglets' before being renamed in 1950. The current name may be grander, but it's now inaccurate; there are only eight of these majestic limestone stacks left – the others have collapsed into the ocean. Nonetheless they remain an impressive sight, especially when buffeted by the heavy seas that are common along the entire coast.

Since a ban on whaling in 1935, southern right whales have slowly returned to the aquamarine waters off the Great Ocean Road. In summer the whales live in the sub-Antarctic, but during winter they migrate north to the 'nursery' just off the coast of Warrnambool to give birth to their calves. The females stay in the nursery for several weeks while their calves build up the strength for the trip back south. Sometimes they swim just hundreds of metres offshore.

The iconic **Twelve Apostles** (main picture) on the Great Ocean Road.

Autumn in **Mount Beauty** (right) on the edge of the Alpine National Park in Victoria's north-east.

Inland, The Grampians – named after mountains in Scotland – are nothing short of wondrous. At the bottom of the Great Dividing Range, these mostly sandstone peaks and ranges stretch for 80 kilometres from north to south, punctuated by waterfalls, lakes, forests and alpine flowers. The area, known as Gariwerd by local Aborigines, has been home to the Jardwadjali and Djab Wurrung people for thousands of years and contains about 60 rock art sites.

Phillip Island is also uniquely beautiful. It boasts incredible landmarks, including an awesome blowhole that spews water into the sky during big southern swells, and Pyramid Rock, an area where 400-million-year-old meets 50-million-year-old basalt, forming a pyramid shaped island. The island is home to possibly the country's most popular wildlife attraction: the Penguin Parade, which happens in the evening when little penguins return from the sea each night and waddle up the beach to their burrows.

Wilsons Promontory, or 'the Prom' as Victorians affectionately call it, has some of the state's most pristine bushland and beaches, including the pure white quartz of Squeaky Beach, which was named for the noise it makes as you walk on it. The park contains a significant habitat of the New Holland mouse and its yanakie grasslands offer ample opportunity for viewing Eastern grey kangaroos, wombats and emus. The Prom also features a restored 1859 granite lighthouse which juts dramatically into the Bass Strait. To stand on it is to feel you are at the wild, beautiful edge of the world.

Toby and Percina the penguins model jumpers that will be sent to Phillip Island to aid any of their kind who get caught in oil spills.

TEN OF THE BEST ... NATIONAL PARKS

The Grampians National Park a paradise for rockclimbing, bushwalking and flower-gazing.

Port Campbell National Park home to the rugged coastline of the Great Ocean Road – one of the best road trips in Australia.

Mornington Peninsula National Park pleasant bay beaches contrasted with windswept coastline on the ocean-side.

Dandenong Ranges home to lyrebirds and rosellas, this park is a favourite weekend haunt for Melbournites.

Snowy River National Park in an area popularised by Banjo Paterson, this is true Aussie wilderness. It is home to the endangered brush-tailed rock wallaby.

Alpine National Park the idyllic high country, popular with skiers in the winter and hikers in the summer.

Wilsons Promontory National Park mainland Australia's southernmost national park, and loved by Victorians for its beautiful rainforests and unspoilt beaches.

The Murray-Sunset National Park a semi-arid area which is remarkably untouched.

Kinglake National Park home to Masons Falls, a popular picnic area with impressive falls and natural flora.

The Hattah-Kulkyne National Park part of the Murray–Mallee region, this park is known for its red dirt and abundant birdlife.

CRIKEY!

Walkers around the lower lakes of the Murray River are well advised to wear sturdy boots – along with the incredible flora and birdlife in the area is some nastier wildlife: the **tiger snake**. The snake, which mostly eats small vertebrates, may feature tiger-like cross-bands on its skin but some sub-species are completely black.

It is considered the most dangerous snake in Australia, and is extremely aggressive when aroused. Its venom attacks the nervous system but death from a bite is rare these days as an antivenene is available.

The **cool Aussie esky**, plastered with stickers of the country's hottest beers.

PICTURECREDITS

Abbreviations: t=top, b=bottom, c=centre, l=left, r=right
COVER Michael Fletcher/AustraliaStockPhotos.com
vi/vii/148 inset Newspix/Leon Mead viii/ix Lonely Planet/Richard Nebesky

NSW x/1 Fairfaxphotos.com/James Brickwood 2 Random House 3 t Random House 3 c Reproduced with the permission of the NSW Government 3 b Newspix/Sandra Priestley 3 National Library of Australia (nla.pic-an6016289) 5 tr Random House 5 tc Random House 5 r Newspix/George Evatt 5 l Newspix/Jeff Darmanin 6 Newspix/Jeff Darmanin 7 Newspix/Toby Zerna 8 Newspix/Marc McCormack 9 Newspix/Scott Hornby 10& 11 Lonely Planet/MT Media 12 t Random House 12 b Random House 13 tr Random House 13 l Random House 13 br Random House 14 National Library of Australia (nla.pic-vn3071984) 15 Newspix/Brendan Read 16 t Random House 16 b Random House 17 t AAP Image/Dave Hodgson 17 br Random House 18 Newspix/Frank Violi 19 Newspix/Justin Lloyd 20 Newspix/Matthew Vasilescu 21 Newspix/Brett Faulkner 22 r Newspix/Jeremy Piper 22 l Newspix/Nick Wilson 23 Newspix/Jason Busch 24 Newspix/James Croucher 25 Newspix/Bob Barker 26/27 Random House 27 b Random House 28 t Newspix/John Grainger 28 b Random House 29 Random House 31 Newspix/Alex Coppel 32/33 Random House 32 tr Lonely Planet Images/Holger Leue 32 br Lonely Planet Images/Claver Carroll 34 Newspix/Sam Mooy 35 Newspix/Paul Trezise 36 tr Newspix/Sarah Rhodes 36 bl Newspix/James Croucher 37 Newspix/Sarah Rhodes 38/39 Newspix/Craig Greenhill 38 tr Random House 39 r Newspix/Sam Ruttyn 39 l Lonely Planet Images/John Borthwick 39 Random House 40 Random House 41 r Random House 41 l Newspix/Angelo Soulas 42 r Newspix/Gregg Porteous 42 l Newspix/Phil Hillyard 43 r Newspix/Gregg Porteous 43 l Newspix/Mark Evans 44 r Lonely Planet Images/Ross Barnett 44 l Random House 45 br Newspix/Marc McCormack 45 Newspix/Jeff Darmanin 46 t Newspix/Chris Hyde 46 bl Random House 47 Newspix/Nathan Edwards 48 Newspix/Sarah Rhodes 49 t Newspix/Alan Pryke 49 b Newspix/Adam Ward 50/51 Random House 51 r Random House 51 c Random House 52/53 Random House 52 t Random House 52 bc Newspix/Bill Rosier

ACT 54/55 Random House 56 National Library of Australia (nla.pic-vn3699709) 57 tl Random House 57 br Lonely Planet/Simon Foale 57 bl Lonely Planet/Jason Edwards 57 Reproduced with the permission of the ACT Government 58 Random House 59 tr Newspix/Kym Smith 59 main pic Lonely Planet/Simon Foale 60 Newspix/John Feder 61 Newspix/Kym Smith 62/63 Lonely Planet/Trevor Creighton 63 t Newspix/Bob Barker 63 b Newspix/Renee Nowytarger 64 Newspix/Ray Strange 65 t AAP Image/Alan Porritt 65 c Lonely Planet/Chris Mellor 65 b Newspix/Gary Ramage

QLD 66/67 Lonely Planet/Holger Leue 68 National Library of Australia (nla.pic-an7878644) 69 t Random House 69 b National Library of Australia (nla.pic-an24229271) 70 Lonely Planet/Lee Foster 71 tr Newspix/David Sproule 71 tl Reproduced with the permission of the Queensland Government 71 br Lonely Planet/Mitch Reardon 71 bl Newspix/Drew Fitzgibbon 71 bcr Gekko/Keir Davis 71 bcr Newspix/David Sproule 72 Newspix/Patrick Hamilton 73 Newspix/Rogato Pasco 74/75 Lonely Planet/Chris Mellor 75 tr Newspix/Tony Phillips 75 br Lonely Planet/David Wall 76/77 Lonely Planet/David Wall 76 bl Newspix/Mark Calleja 78/79 Lonely Planet/Richard I'Anson 78 Lonely Planet/David Wall 80 Newspix/Paul Riley 82/83 Newspix/Craig Greenhill 82 l Gekko/Barbara Bryan Photography 84/85 Random House 84 t Newspix/Jamie Hanson 85 tr Random House 85 tl Random

House 86 Newspix/Bob Fenney 87 tr Newspix/Anthony Weate 87 bl Gekko/Nick Rains 88 Newspix/David Sproule 89 r Newspix/Geoff McLachlan 89 r Newspix/Warwick Quest 89 l Gekko/Matt Wilson 89 l State Library of Queensland 90/91 Newspix/Darren England 91 r Newspix/Wayne McLachlan 92 Newspix/Steve Pohlner 93 Lonely Planet/John Banagan 94 Newspix/Nathan Richter 95 t Newspix/Mark Evans 95 br Newspix/Bill Mcauley 96/97 Newspix/Antony Weate 96 l Newspix/Derek Moore 97 r Newspix/Marc Robertson 98 tl Lonely Planet/Paul Dymond 98 br Newspix/Anthony Weate 99 Newspix/Eddie Safarik 100 Newspix/Michael Marschall 101 tr Lonely Planet/Michael Aw 101 l Lonely Planet/Holger Leue 101 br Newspix/Cameron Laird 102/103 Random House 103 br Newspix/Patrina Malone 103 bl Random House 104 Random House 105 Newspix/Mark Cranitch

NT 106/107 Lonely Planet/Ross Barnett 108 r National Library of Australia (nla.pic-an 11360266-74) 108 l Newspix 109 Newspix Newspix/Michael Marschall 111 tr reproduced with the permission of the Northern Territory Government 111 tl Gekko/Bio-Images 111 cl Gekko/Dennis Jones 111 br Lonely Planet/Christopher Groenhout 111 ll Lonely Planet/Martin Cohen 112/113 Newspix/James Croucher 113 tr Newspix/Chris Hyde 113 br Lonely Planet/Michael Gebicki 114/115 Lonely Planet/Will Salter 114 tr Lonely Planet/John Banagan 116 t Newspix 116 bl Newspix/Brad Fleet 117 Newspix/Lyndon Mechielson 118 r Lonely Planet/Regis Martin 118 l Newspix 119 Newspix/Michael Marschall 120 Lonely Planet/Michael Gebicki 121 Random House 122 Newspix/Lyndon Mechielson 123 tl Newspix/Brett Hartwig 123 br Newspix/Dani Gawlik 124 Random House 125 Newspix/Alex Coppel 126 Lonely Planet/Oliver Strewe 128 r Random House 128 l Lonely Planet/Martin Cohen 129 Newspix/Eddie Safarik

WA 130/131 Lonely Planet/Christopher Groenhout 132 tr National Library of Australia (nla.pic-an8134721) 132 bl Random House 134/135 Newspix/Bruce Magilton 135 tr Newspix/Jody D'arcy 135 tl Reproduced with the permission of the Western Australian Government 135 br Newspix 135 bl Newspix/Ernie McLintock 136 Newspix 137 Newspix/Lyndon Mechielson 138/139 Gekko/Rob Walls 138 t Lonely Planet/Wayne Walton 139 tr Lonely Planet/Peter Ptschelinzew 140/141 Newspix/Stewart Allen 141 tl Newspix/Tom Rovis-Herrmann 142 Newspix/Karin Calvert-Borshoff 143 Lonely Planet/Peter Ptschelinzew 144 Random House 145 Newspix/Ian Cugley 146 Newspix/Stewart Allen 147 Lonely Planet/Peter Ptschelinzew 148/149 Lonely Planet/Peter Ptschelinzew 150/151 Newspix/Megan Lewis 152 Newspix/Megan Lewis 153 t Newspix/Jody D'arcy 154/155 Newspix/Ian Munro 156 Newspix/Jackson Flindell 156 Newspix/Jody D'arcy 159 Lonely Planet/Richard I'Anson 160 Newspix/Richard Polden 161 Newspix/Elke Wiesman 162/163 Lonely Planet/Richard I'Anson 163 tr Random House 164/165 Newspix/Nathan Richter 166/167 Random House 166 l Lonely Planet/Martin Cohen 168 Lonely Planet/Mitch Reardon 169 main pic Lonely Planet/Richard I'Anson 169 l Random House

SA 170/171 Newspix/Nicholas Wrankmore 172 Newspix 173 tr Random House 174 Newspix/Lindsay Moller 175 tr Newspix/Lindsay Moller 175 tc Reproduced with the permission of the SA Government 175 cr Random House 175 cl Random House 175 br Newspix/Craig Borrow 175 bl Lonely Planet/Jason Edwards 177 main pic Newspix/Sam Mooy 177 inset Newspix 179 r Lonely Planet/Ross Barnett 179 l Lonely Planet/Christopher Groenhout 180 Gekko/Adam North 181 Newspix/Trish Johnson 182 t Newspix/Naomi Jellicoe 182 b Newspix/Lindsay Moller 183 Lonely Planet/Chris Mellor 184/185 Lonely Planet/Michael Gebicki 184 l Newspix 186

Lonely Planet/Mitch Reardon 187 tl Newspix/Ben Searcy 187 br Random House 188/189 Newspix/Stephen Laffer 189 Newspix/James Elsby 190 Newspix 191 Newspix/Sam Mooy 192 t Lonely Planet/Diana Mayfield 192 b Newspix/Ray Titus 194/195 Lonely Planet/Richard I'Anson 194 c Lonely Planet/Diana Mayfield 196 Newspix/James Elsby 197 t Newspix/Jo-Anna Robinson 197 b Newspix/Dean Martin 198/199 Lonely Planet/Richard I'Anson 198 r Random House 199 r Lonely Planet/Holger Leue 200 Random House 201 Newspix/Greg Adams 202/203 Lonely Planet/Richard I'Anson 202 r Newspix/Sam Mooy 202 l Random House 202 c Random House 204/205 Newspix/Matthew Newton

TAS 206 National Library of Australia (nla.pic-an2288513) 207 b National Library of Australia (nla.pic-an23594157) 208 Lonely Planet/Rob Blakers 209 r Lonely Planet/Regis Martin 209 lc Gekko/Steve Lovegrove 209 bl Random House 209 bc Gekko/Bio-Images 208 t Reproduced with the permission of the Tasmanian government 211 r Newspix/David Geraghty 211 l Newspix/Nathan Edwards 212/213 b Gekko/Ian Wallace 212 tl Lonely Planet/Richard I'Anson 212 c Newspix/Matthew Newton 213 br Newspix/Amy Brown 214/215 b Gekko/Ian Wallace 214 l Newspix/Chris Kidd 215 r Random House 216/217 Newspix/Mark Williams 217 t Lonely Planet/Peter Hendrie 217 c Newspix/Matthew Newton 217 b Newspix/Jason Busch 218 Newspix/Sam Rosewarne 219 Lonely Planet/Holger Leue 220/221 Newspix 220 bl Newspix/Renee Nowytarger 221 tr Lonely Planet/Andrew Bain 221 t Random House 221 bl Newspix/Ross Marsden 221 b Random House 222/223 Lonely Planet/Rob Blakers 224 main pic Lonely Planet/Rob Blakers 224 inset Newspix/Peter Mathew 225 Lonely Planet/John Hay

VIC 226/227 Lonely Planet/James Braund 228 Newspix 229 r National Library of Australia (nla.pic-an2377132) 230 Gekko/Andrew Chapman 231 tl Newspix/Ben Swinnerton 231 t Reproduced with the permission of the Victorian Government 231 cr Gekko/Bio-Images 231 cl Newspix/Simone Dalton 231 br Gekko/Ian Wallace 231 bl Gekko/Bio-Images 232 tr Lonely Planet/Dallas Stribley 232 bl Newspix/Leader/Maria Reed 233 Newspix/Colleen Petch 234 Newspix 235 Newspix/Wayne Ludbey 236/237 Gekko/Nick Rains 236 Lonely Planet/James Braund 238 Lonely Planet/Juliet Coombe 239 r Lonely Planet/John Banagan 239 l Gekko/Andrew Chapman 240 t Gekko/Vito Vampatella 240 bl Newspix/Michael Potter 241 Lonely Planet/Juliet Coombe 242/243 Newspix/David Caird 242 Newspix/Stuart McEvoy 243 Lonely Planet/Richard I'Anson 246 t Newspix/Norm Oorloff 246 b Vue de Monde/Earl Carter 247 t Vue de Monde/Tim James 247 b Newspix/Dean Cambray 248 Lonely Planet/Paul Sinclair 249 t Lonely Planet/James Braund 249 b Gekko/magoo on safari 250/251 Gekko/Dennis Jones 251 r Lonely Planet/Krzysztof Dydynsk 252 Lonely Planet/Bernard Napthine 252 Newspix/David Crosling 254 t Gekko/Heath Worsley Imagery 254 b Random House 255 Newspix/Eamon Gallagher 256/257 Newspix/Trevor Pinder 258/259 Gekko/Andrew Chapman 258 l Newspix/Greg Scullin 260/261 Newspix/Kelly Barnes 260 l Newspix/Michael Klein 262 t Newspix/Rob Leeson 262 br Newspix/Kelly Barnes 262 bl Newspix/Darren McNamara 263 Newspix/Craig Borrow 264 Newspix/Phil Hillyard 365 br Newspix/Wayne Ludbey 265 tl Newspix/Michael Dodge 266 Newspix/Mike Keating 267 t Newspix/David Geraghty 267 bl Lonely Planet/Juliet Coombe 268 Newspix/Paul Trezise 269 Lonely Planet/Krzysztof Dydynski 270 l Newspix/Fiona Hamilton 270 b Newspix/Andrew MacColl 271 tl Newspix/Cameron Tandy 271 main pic Newspix/Adam Smith 272/273 Gekko/Paul Pennell 273 br Random House 274 Newspix/Toby Zerna 275 Newspix/Bill Mcauley
END PAGE 276/277 Lonely Planet/Claver Carroll

Random House Australia Pty Ltd
Level 3, 100 Pacific Highway, North Sydney, NSW 2060
www.randomhouse.com.au

Sydney   New York   Toronto
London   Auckland   Johannesburg

First published by Random House Australia 2007

Copyright © Random House Australia Pty Ltd, 2007

National Library of Australia
Cataloguing-in-Publication Entry

Australia today.

ISBN 978 1 74166 576 5 (hbk.).

1. Australia – Description and travel – 2001–.
2. Australia – Civilisation – 2001–. I. Title.

919.4

Cover photograph 'Ningaloo' by Michael Fletcher/AustraliaStockPhotos.com
Cover design by Saso Content & Design Pty Ltd
Internal design by Saso Content & Design Pty Ltd
Printed and bound by Imago

10 9 8 7 6 5 4 3 2 1